FECKLESS JUDGES

FECKLESS JUDGES

Oliver Kaye

AuthorHouse™
1663 Liberty Drive
Bloomington, IN 47403
www.authorhouse.com
Phone: 1-800-839-8640

First published by AuthorHouse 02/17/2012

ISBN: 978-1-4678-8472-3 (sc)
ISBN: 978-1-4678-8473-0 (ebk)

Printed in the United States of America

This book is printed on acid-free paper.

Cover illustration by Jeffrey Wright

CONTENTS

Chapter One

The Legal System

This book has been written after a very sad painful experience that has led me to believe that the British legal system does not exist per se. Even though there have been considerable reforms over the last thirty years, only England and Wales share common law and procedures. Scotland and Northern Ireland have different systems. The Family Law Division covers divorce and separation and matters concerning children and parenting. In general terms, the bulk of the court's work is divided between civil and criminal work. There are several other courts in the system such as the Ecclesiastical Court. I became embroiled with both the civil and criminal court system.

In the Magistrates court all civil cases are heard and tried by an officer of the justice system, a lay magistrate, district, circuit or high court judge. There are no juries except in the Criminal Crown Court and the Criminal High Court. The Magistrate's Court hears minor criminal cases such as my alleged common assault. If, in the system, you are unhappy with a judgement you have to get a more senior judge to hear an appeal. Generally this means going to a higher court, all the way up to the Supreme Court of England and Wales.

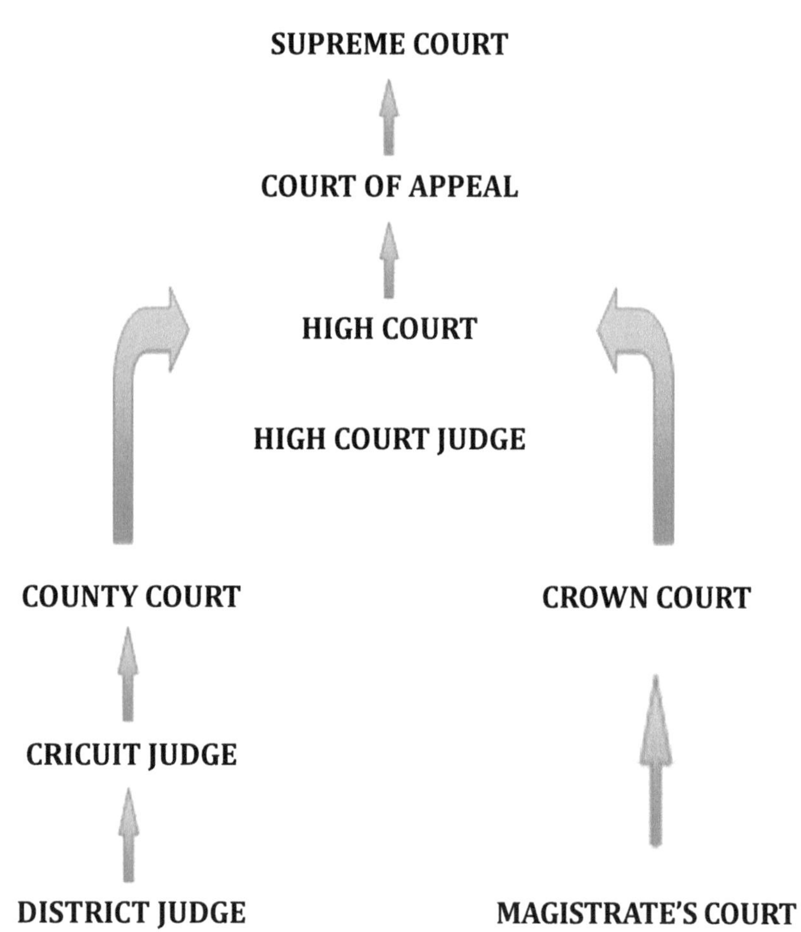

CIVIL
(Family law)
CRIMINAL
SUPREME COURT
COURT OF APPEAL
HIGH COURT
HIGH COURT JUDGE
COUNTY COURT
CROWN COURT
CRICUIT JUDGE
DISTRICT JUDGE
MAGISTRATE'S COURT

Confusingly following the reorganisation of the system that took place not long ago, some Magistrate's Courts now have Family Proceedings Courts sitting alongside the normal business of the court. These deal with Public Law cases.

A district judge, then a circuit judge and finally a high court judge hear the bottom tier in the county courts, Family Division. In the High Court there are various "circuits". High court judges are based at the Royal Courts of Justice in the Strand in London. They travel to regional jurisdictions to hear cases at the local County Courts. The court that hears your case originally is chosen on the basis that it is the nearest to where your children normally reside. In my case that was in the Thames Valley, so we started at the Newbury Court. When the case was elevated to the High Court, the hearings were arranged where the judge had the first available time slot. That could be at any County Court on his circuit or "bench". I had hearings at Newbury and Reading.

Getting Involved with the Court

How do you get involved with the courts? In order to get divorced you have to get a court order from a judge to dissolve the marriage. First, you get a Decree Nisi, when everything is agreed in principle. Then the administrative cogs whirr for several months before you are granted a Decree Absolute. This is the formal dissolution of the marriage. You can apply to represent yourself in court as a Litigant In Person (LIP), or pay a solicitor to represent you. In contested situations where the two sides are at war you will probably require a barrister, sometimes referred to as 'counsel', to represent you in the court. You need a solicitor to engage a barrister. In 2001 I was told if I could get an amicable agreement with my wife I could expect the cost of my proceedings to be about £5,000. If I wanted to argue and contest things in court, I was told, it could easily escalate to £20,000 or more. It turned out to cost me more than £200,000. Divorce where children are involved is split into two areas: Child Matters and Ancillary Relief. The latter is basically the financial agreement and boils down to maintenance for one party or a clean break financially and the division of any possessions. Both the financial arrangements and the division of possessions can be very stressful and emotional negotiations. If you cannot agree the judge will impose his judgement. Child maintenance is by negotiation, but is underpinned by legal minimum levels dependant on the number of children involved and the income level of the non-resident parent that contributes. If there are problems over payment then this comes under the management of the Child Support Agency, who have draconian powers to force payments.

Choosing a Solicitor

How do you choose a solicitor? A starting point is to make sure they are either a member of the Solicitors Family Law Association or Association of Lawyers for Children. I know of no reliable way to gauge how good a solicitor is. Personal recommendation is fine if you know a lot about the case involved. Cases like mine involving extreme alienation are thankfully not that common. Most divorces are negotiated relatively amicably, or the disputes are narrowed down, usually to one area. Where, in effect, one partner declares all out war on the other and uses the child or children involved to hurt or humiliate the other, the chances of selecting a brilliant solicitor and barrister are very slim. If you use a large firm, junior staff, overseen by a more experienced solicitor, tend to do most of the work. If you use a small firm you run the risk of dealing with a lack of available experience or skill. My first solicitor and barrister were simply not experienced enough. Making a choice by fee rating is not a sound way to choose a solicitor. I am sceptical of firms that have expensive, swanky offices; their advice will probably be no better than more down to earth firms. My first firm was a small town practise. My second firm were based over 80 miles from my home. My first solicitor used a barrister from chambers in Portsmouth, the second firm used a London chambers. Barristers travel to wherever the hearing is.

The truth is that until you have been in the system a while it is extremely difficult to gauge whether the advice you receive is good, poor or even correct! With my first barrister I found I just could not agree with his strategy or some of his advice. But I assumed that he knew what he was talking about, especially as I was paying a lot for his expertise. My gut feelings turned out to be correct. Later I paid more attention to my gut feelings.

Some of the things I was told by my first solicitor were simply untrue. I was told that I had to use a barrister from certain chambers. In fact you can use any barrister you choose. What is true is that you have to instruct a barrister through a solicitor. It was explained that this has something to do with insurance. It is too expensive for a barrister to insure himself to act directly for you. I was told that whomsoever lost a case was liable to pay all or a proportion of the costs as decided by the judge. As the years went by, no matter how bad my wife's behaviour got in delaying and frustrating proceedings, I had to continually pay my costs to bring her back to court. I had over 50 hearings, yet I was awarded the costs (reimbursement) from only two small hearings. Recently a Queen's Counsel (QC) advised me that in private law each side pays their own costs; usually only costs of lost appeals are awarded against you.

Child Matters

Child Matters is the agreement or the apportionment of time spent by the children with each parent and determines who has primary care of them. My parents divorced reasonably civilly. My mother was granted everything unchallenged on the understanding that my father could see us up to half the time in the holidays. Apart from a few niggles, that trust between them and with their children's best interests at heart, was enough for it to work. When one partner tries to exclude the other, as in my case, over time the legal process gets ever more detailed and complicated. The two main areas of conflict that arise are over residency and contact. In my case these both became subject to court orders. Whether the allegations brought to destroy the other parent's right to see the children are based on fact or are spurious, the judge will ask for outside agencies to provide background reports to aid in making the right orders.

CAFCASS

The commonest agency in private law is Cafcass: the children and family court advisory and support service. They used to be part of the probationary service, but are now accountable to the Secretary of State for Education. Their role is to safeguard and promote the welfare of the children, give advice to the family court, make provision for the children to be represented, and to provide information, advice and support to children and their families.

To my mind a Cafcass officer is a social worker by another name. They produce reports on a child's family background, living arrangements, schooling and relationships with both parents. If the case becomes protracted the judge may elevate the officer to the position of Court Guardian for the child. In this role the Cafcass officer now appointed Court Guardian allows the child to have separate legal representation. The Guardian also has more powers to get information and cooperation from other agencies, such as Social Services. In theory the Cafcass officer, and especially in the role of Guardian, is the most influential person for the judge. It is his or her job to advise the judge. The advisors at Families Need Fathers recommend very strongly that you do not cross swords with the Cafcass officer.

Barristers

The law is extremely complicated and there are nasty traps for the unwary. I found, from experience with many barristers that it was almost impossible to find one that was a good all-rounder. For example he or she might be a very good strategist but hopeless at talking in front of the judge. Or they might be good on the primary case but poor at fighting for costs. The annoying thing is that you do not know how good your barrister is until he/she performs in front of the judge. You can actually use a solicitor to represent you in court, in many cases. Unless you negotiate differently with the solicitor they work on an hourly billing system. They have to declare their fees for all the different aspects of their work before you engage them. The barrister operates on a per hearing basis. They quote for representing you for the day in court, whether they go before the judge for a whole day or just 15 minutes. Their quotes include the cost of travel, accommodation, if necessary and preparation time. In my experience they worked out cheaper than the solicitor at court. You can spend hours sitting waiting at the court. The judge will usually have several other cases to attend to on the same day, unless it is booked out as a final hearing and there are no emergency applications to hear. The judge sits from 10 am, has an hour for lunch and usually goes between 4 and 5pm. You may hang around for three hours and then go before the judge for as little as 15 minutes. Most courts have small consulting rooms for private discussion with your legal team. But if there are several cases before the judge you may have to discuss your case in the corridor or general waiting area, sometimes in full view and hearing of the opposition. I always turned up early to make sure I got a consulting room. I think it is an unnecessary expense to have both a solicitor and barrister at court. Usually I refused to allow my solicitor to attend, except for a final hearing.

Hearings

There are different types of hearings. After the initial hearing the judge may order a review hearing to see how things are progressing. There may be a Directions hearing when an issue is to be aired, possibly being resolved with an order. These will eventually lead to a trial or final hearing. There may be a pre-trial review beforehand to iron out any procedural problems, so being unprepared does not waste the trial time. You do not have to attend these, unless you are LIP. You attend all other hearings, but you are unlikely to be called upon to speak. In general you do not speak in court, your barrister does. Sometimes you are required to produce a position statement. This is outlining, sometimes detailed, what you want or how you want things to proceed. It should be short, no more than a few pages. The judge will read these before the hearing so that he has an idea of what is to be considered on the day. Before substantive hearings such as the final hearing you will be asked to produce a written statement or affidavit, along with the same for any witnesses you intend to use. These are signed under oath. They have to be lodged with the court within set procedural deadlines; so the other parties have time to read and study them. A frequent dirty trick my wife's legal team employed was to hand these over late, sometimes at the hearing itself. This left little time to respond effectively. If you are LIP there are web sites you can pay to access for all the procedural details.

At a trial or final hearing you will be asked to take the stand and swear an oath. Your barrister or counsel will ask you questions, then the other counsels will question you. Sometimes the judge may ask questions too. The same applies to the experts in the case, if called to report, and any witnesses to be heard. You may be cross-examined again if the judge feels the situation warrants it and if there is time. Generally speaking you will be questioned on the details in your statement. For their part, the opposition will attempt to find discrepancies or cast doubt on what you say.

When you are in court, and in legal documents, you will be referred to as the applicant or (co) respondent. Although my wife started the divorce proceedings, they were in go-slow mode to delay a hearing to discuss contact. So in an effort to kick-start the proceedings, I sued for divorce. As I had brought the action I was called the applicant. My wife was the respondent, and my son later joined as co or joint respondent. The applicant's legal team has the management of the case before the court. They handle all the filing of statements, documents and the hearing "bundle" before the judge. They are responsible for organising the case outline chronology, and the bundle, which is the file or files available with copies to everyone in court so that the judge can refer to a document and everyone can find it at the same place in the bundle of documents. My last final hearing bundle consisted of two arch files containing over 800 pages. This places extra costs on the applicant. There has to be a level of consensus on what goes into the bundle, so more letters fly around. When my ex-wife and myself were both LIP, the judge ordered my son's solicitor to take control of the case as the only professional remaining. As a minor my son was legally aided.

Charges and Legal Aid

My wife was on a publicly funded certificate, i.e. legal aid. Legally aided cases seem to be the preserve of the big firms now. Fewer firms offer to act for legally aided clients, as there is so little profit for them. As a result very junior staff do most of the work. There are irritating little tricks they use to boost profitability. Letters are charged at a fixed rate. So whilst my solicitor may ask several questions or raise different issues in one letter, the legal aid firm will only address one issue or question per letter; so requiring several letters. All of these required my solicitor to answer, increasing my costs too. If you have fixed assets such as a house, the legal aid board will put a charge on the property. In the event that the house is sold the legal aid board will have first call on any money owed, even before a bank. The legal aid is in effect deferred; in the meantime you pay interest on the money owed. If you have no assets, then legal aid is, in effect, free. In my experience legal aid is open to abuse. There are rules governing who is eligible to claim. In a separate case involving a neighbour and a right of way dispute I complained that he should not be eligible for legal aid. I provided a detailed submission as to why. The legal aid board's response was that the amount involved did not warrant investigation. Even though it amounted to tens of thousands of pounds. As my solicitor put it, if you falsify your application, nobody checks up. My wife inexplicably got legal aid till she lost her appeal: when the legal aid board said it was no longer in the public interest to support her case.

The Expert Witness

If you are unlucky enough to have to progress through the system, there will probably come a point when you will encounter an expert witness, or indeed have to call on one. It seems to me that once a professional has advised the court in any way, when giving evidence on future occasions, they can then attach the moniker "expert". But this is not a declaration of knowledge or experience as such. When perusing the C.V.s of these professionals you will probably encounter descriptions like "experienced in Public Law cases". Within Family Law there are Public and Private Law cases. Public law cases are where the State is involved, usually through Social Services. These are often cases that involve emergency protection, care and supervision, secure accommodation etc. Private law cases like mine are conducted between individuals and are about residence (custody), contact and parental responsibility.

When I went before senior judges I was surprised to find that they required expert's advice. I expected their level of experience to lessen the need for such experts. I also assumed a degree of training in child psychology or at least a thorough understanding gained over the years. What I found was that there seems to be an unnecessary level of extra cost imposed on the system, bringing in these so called experts, rather than a reliance on a judge's own experience or expertise in Child Matters. Maybe senior judges should be better trained?

The English and Welsh do not have a Bill of Rights or a written constitution. Our laws have evolved out of and with common law—new ones being crafted in Parliament. In our adversarial system laws are interpreted, adapted or amended through the very slow process of appeals up to the highest level, where if successful, they become "precedent".

In the modern era, as society changes at an ever-increasing pace, the law and its interpretation lag far behind. The nation is now a signatory to the European Convention of Human Rights and is no longer sovereign but under the auspices of the European Court. Over time our system will have to merge with the European model, assuming the European Union vision remains intact. At present much of our law is based on the Children's Act of 1989. This applies to children under 18 years of age.

The Police

The agency I had most contact with was the police, because my wife alleged all sorts of domestic violence early on. I came up against some shocking bias in my dealings with this branch of the law. I was arrested twice for alleged common assault. When the case came before the Magistrate's court, it was dismissed. When I eventually received an apology from the police for the way I had been treated, I was told they had responded to 22 calls to visit the farmhouse. What completely stunned me was their admission that they had Home Office guidelines to arrest on the third call out for domestic violence allegations, even if they did not believe the allegations! To be fair they did acknowledge early on that they thought there was something not quite right about the allegations and delayed arresting me at the third call out. But even although my wife's behaviour gave me cause to phone them on several occasions they declined to respond except once when they arrested me and a second time when I had to ring them three times in an hour to get my wife to move her vehicle which she had parked to block the driveway to prevent me leaving the property for good as I was attempting to do, on the orders of a judge. The treatment was also very different. The local police sergeant advised me in no uncertain terms that in calls about domestic violence I simply could not win in any situation. All the incidents would be used to produce a convincing argument for the court as to why I should be denied contact with my son. His phrase was "been there, done that, got the tee shirt. Walk away or get out". Over breeches of contact orders the police never once told my wife to comply, even when presented with the order! I was told to leave or be arrested! The only exception was an occasion when I insisted on taping the conversation; then they were more balanced. The message was very loud and very clear: if I broke a court order I would be arrested. If my wife broke a court order I had to refer the matter back to court. (With the inevitable 3-month delay).

By chance I learnt that my local police had a domestic violence liaison officer. She was very sympathetic to my predicament. She explained, after my second arrest, that if I kept her informed of the incidents of domestic violence, the local police would have a better understanding of the situation and may present a more balanced approach. She also explained that the government definition of domestic violence had completely changed. It now included incidents of non-violent abuse, ranging from denial of contact to verbal abuse. Over the years I logged all manner of abuse by my wife/ ex-wife as domestic violence. If more men registered the abuse metered out to them, then the national statistics would not look so one-sided.

Litigant in Person (LIP) and the McKenzie Friend

If you want to represent yourself in court as an LIP, you have to inform the court that you want to do this. Personally I am very uncomfortable speaking in public, so I found the process very daunting. There is a strong opinion at Families Need Fathers and other support groups that being LIP is the only sensible option. I never expected that the judges would allow my case to run and run, so I had not expected to pay out over £200,000 for legal work. If I had known at the beginning what I know now, I would have been LIP from the start. It is daunting, but you may engage a McKenzie Friend to help. Originally a McKenzie Friend was a volunteer helper/advisor who is allowed to sit in court with the permission of the judge. He/she does not engage in the process and cannot speak in court. He/she can help by taking notes or giving advice during the hearing. My McKenzie Friend decided to turn the knowledge he had accrued into a business opportunity. He had been on many legal courses alongside lawyers. He offered his advice at about half the cost of my solicitor's firm. He wanted to act as an unqualified lawyer for me, but I declined. He accompanied me to one hearing as a paid McKenzie friend. He continued as a paid advisor for a while, and then generously gave his advice for free. If I had had access to a book like this before I started my epic struggle I know without a doubt that I could have saved myself a huge amount of money. He opened my eyes to the archaic procedures and protocols of the court. There is an amazing amount of information on the web, but you need to know how to access it and filter it. When I first met my McKenzie friend through Families Need Fathers, I did not even know how to send an email! He was shocked! He communicated only via email and in an emergency, by text. I am grateful that he forced me to learn some basic skills with the computer. If you do become LIP it is important that you keep copies of, most importantly, the court bundle and correspondence over any issues. All the expert reports, court orders, statements and chronology will be in the court bundle. After seven years my solicitor said they had 22 files of paperwork on my case. It is staggering and quite ridiculous, the avalanche of paper produced by the legal system. Towards the end of my involvement with the courts it was quite a challenge to physically turn up at court with all the necessary documents in a holdall, especially if I had parked somewhere less expensive than the centre of town, where the court is usually located and to walk with my heavy load!

There are always tight security measures at the county courts. There is always a metal detector scanner and you can always expect a search of your cases. You register at reception to find out which court you are to appear in. Then you go to the area around that court. Eventually the court usher will appear and advise you as to when you might go before the judge. Very often the legal teams will discuss the case beforehand and try to do a deal. Invariably the usher will pop round to see if any deals have been struck or any progress made. He will report back to the judge. Sometimes a judge will order a recess for everyone to negotiate a solution, and make it clear that he will not welcome a return until the problem is sorted.

Residence, the modern term for custody, is an area fraught with hypocrisy and double standards. It seems to me that in the eyes of the law both parents are supposed to start from an equal basis. In practice though, and certainly in my experience, in the eyes of the court, the only parent that matters is the primary carer. The guidance policy from the government is that the default setting should be a "no residence order". Many people talk about a shared residence order as being ideal. Shared residency can only be given if the child actively spends nights at each home. If the child is very young and still being breast-fed then this is plainly not possible. Personally I feel a new category, shared parenting (joint custody) would be far more satisfactory: even though one parent may still be categorised as the primary carer. If parents live in different areas, then the child will have to spend more time with the one living in the area in which the child goes to school. That, I believe, should not effectively relegate the other parent to being seen as second class, but it does. Outside of the court the various agencies are only interested in who has residence. If there is no residence order, then they will ask who the primary carer is. The primary carer has a de-facto residence order. It is a cruel reality that whomsoever has residence is the only important parent at ground level in eyes of the public agencies like the police and social services. The parental rights of the non-resident or second-class parent are ignored, and in many instances actively denied. On several occasions I had to get my solicitor to educate social workers, police officers and the staff of the doctor's surgery of my rights to basic information about my son. In some cases the Social Services had advised other professionals not to release information to me, in contravention of the law. It is extraordinary the lack of knowledge about this in the public agencies, or is it just a carefully cultivated bias?

Chapter Two

Getting Involved with the Court

How do you get involved with the courts? Well probably the only time that most of us have to become involved with the courts is in order to get divorced. Then you have to get a court order from a judge to dissolve the marriage. First, you get a Decree Nisi, when everything is agreed in principle. Then the administrative cogs whirr for several months before you are granted a Decree Absolute. This is the formal dissolution of the marriage. You can apply to represent yourself in court as a Litigant In Person (LIP), or pay a solicitor to represent you. In contested situations where the two sides are at war you will probably require a barrister, sometimes referred to as 'counsel,' to represent you in the court. You need a solicitor to engage a barrister. In 2001 I was told if I could get an amicable agreement with my wife I could expect the cost of my proceedings to be about £5,000. If I wanted to argue and contest things in court, I was told, it could easily escalate to £20,000 or more. Divorce, where children are involved is split into two areas: Child Matters and Ancillary Relief. The latter is basically the financial agreement and boils down to maintenance for one party or a clean break financially and the division of any possessions. Both the financial arrangements and the division of possessions can be very stressful and emotional negotiations. If you cannot agree the judge will impose his judgement. Child maintenance is by negotiation, but is underpinned by legal minimum levels dependant on the number of children involved and the income level of the non-resident parent that contributes. If there are problems over payment then this comes under the management of the Child Support Agency, who have draconian powers to force payments.

My first real dealings with the court came soon after Emma and I had moved into the farm when the neighbouring farmer, Elijah Hicks became unpleasant. When we were buying the property it was apparent that there were several documented agricultural rights of way to various outlying fields. My neighbouring dairy farmer blocked off the access to a field of ours. He was not interested in discussing the matter, so I blocked his access across my fields. We quickly found that his local reputation as the village bully and all round neighbourhood nuisance was correct. He tried to use his JCB digger to open up his access. I prevented him by refusing to move out of his way, so he assaulted me. When I defended myself and refused to be intimidated, he got back in his digger and drove straight at me. I picked up a metal fencing bar I had hidden in the hedge and rammed it through the radiator grill of his tractor. Realising that he did not have long before his radiator leaked all it's fluid and the engine would overheat he drove back to his farmyard and called the police. The police did not want to get involved with the rights or wrongs of the situation, and kept saying as it was a civil matter it was for the courts to sort out. So they asked for our assurances to leave the matter with solicitors and to uphold the peace, then they left. With the assurances I felt confident to go and do the milking. Whilst I was milking the neighbour rang a contractor to bulldoze the obstruction. After milking I went to check the damage. Emma had gone ahead. I saw that Elijah Hicks had driven up the short cut right of way, but Emma was holding the gate shut so he could not get back out. He would have to go round the long way. I watched him knock Emma to the ground. So I bellowed at him as I ran to confront him. He leapt into his Landrover and drove off. I was livid. Emma talked some sense into me to ignore it because of the police warning to keep the peace. From the practical point of view I was the only one who could milk the goats and sheep, so getting arrested would just complicate things even more. A few days later I received a summons and eventually after lots of delays by Elijah Hicks we ended up in court to sort the matter. In the meantime we had to endure petty vandalism from him and his children. In the process we discovered that he had had court cases with two other neighbouring farmers and nearly every resident in the hamlet had, at some point, exchanged solicitor's letters over some petty matter. One of his favourite tricks to annoy residents was to spill cow slurry around their boundary or driveway on a regular basis. With us he sprayed slurry across the hedge alongside our yoghurt processing building. We involved the local environmental health department, who intervened to caution him. A few years later he developed motor neurone disease and died. It is a very unpleasant way to die. It was a commonly expressed sentiment in the hamlet that he got natural justice.

Early on in my struggle I stumbled across a letter from our bank. After breakfast in the kitchen I was cleaning the crumbs around the bread bin and moved it. Behind the bread bin I found a letter from the bank dated a month earlier with the information that my signatory and mandate had been duly removed as requested by Mrs Richards. In future the bank would honour no cheques, signed by me. I was thunderstruck at such duplicity, with Emma for keeping it secret from me for a month and with the bank for doing such a thing without consulting me first. Later when my solicitor challenged the bank they responded that they were prepared to defend their legal actions in court if necessary. But in all the time since, up to and including barristers, everyone has remarked that they did not think that a bank could do what my bank did.

It was about this time that the penny finally dropped—Emma would fight no holds barred to get what she wanted. I finally understood what I was up against. When she finally agreed to speak to me, Emma insisted on taping our conversation in the living room. I tried to discuss our short-term future. In the end I said I needed a cheque so I could engage a solicitor to respond to her divorce proceedings. She refused to give me the company chequebook and became verbally abusive and physically tried to remove the spare chequebook when I found that. She threatened to call the police. When I told her to do so, she had second thoughts. I compromised by saying that I would only take one cheque if she promised not to interfere with it. I also wanted £100 cash. Emma threatened to call her solicitor and stop the cheque in the morning. The legal fight was on.

On the day of our first hearing I got up early. Charlie and Emma seemed unhurried. I smelled a rat. I turned up at court and met my barrister, a pleasant lady from the local chambers. We went before a District judge who reminded me very much of Betty Boothroyd, the former Speaker of the House of Commons, she was a very forceful, no nonsense type of lady. The judge realised eventually that Emma was not going to appear. I stuck my hand up like a weaselly schoolboy and asked if I could speak. "No Mr Richards, you only speak when you are spoken to", was the sharp reply. Even my barrister had a hard time getting a word in. The judge was flicking through the documents when her demeanour changed visibly when she asked aloud if the police had been involved. We confirmed that they had in Emma's numerous attempts to accuse me of all sorts of things. Any neutrality died. She adjourned the proceedings for two weeks.

My solicitor and I had the distinct impression that Emma's petition for divorce was being conducted in slow motion. It was explained to me that in order to see Charlie I had to apply for a contact order. This seemed pretty bizarre as I was living in the same house as my son! I could not apparently apply for an order until the divorce action was formally started. I was told Emma could delay things easily. I was advised to petition for divorce myself. I was also advised that it was not possible to add new parts to the petition later; so if I might at some point in the future feel it necessary to ask the court for Charlie to come and live with me, then I had to have it on the starting documents. Although I still thought, at that stage, that Emma would calm down and act reasonably for Charlie's benefit, I did not, in all truth, think that Charlie would be better off with me. Like most people I thought a young child would be better off with his or her mother unless there was a danger of serious abuse. Having said that I wanted considerable contact. I certainly did not expect Emma to go on to abuse Charlie in the way that she has.

The contact hearing came up two weeks after the adjourned first hearing. A detailed schedule of contact was drawn up, with contact for an hour or more every day. The next day Emma was very abusive and obnoxious. She denied contact for several days. Although we were living together in the same house we were separate. I usually waited to use the kitchen after Emma had finished. Emma was always ordering me to clean up after her and do her shopping etc. Of course

I ignored her. I would be told when I could use the washing machine or take the dogs for a walk. It was all very petty but designed to wind me up. My solicitor advised me early on not to become violent, whatever the provocation, as that would completely destroy any court action. It became obvious that Emma's objective was to get me so wound up that I lashed out. She tried very hard all the time I lived in the house. It would never have happened as when I get angry I walk away. I did find it very difficult to endure the constant verbal abuse and petty actions, simply because there was no effective way of combating them or getting them stopped, short of moving out. I could not afford to move out as Emma gave me no money from the business. I borrowed money from my sister Laurie. She was a Godsend and a rock of support, especially in the early years. As she is a professional counsellor, she gave me lots of good advice as well. The impact on my health was terrible. I had a history of Ulcerative Colitis that eventually resulted in cancer of the colon. My colon and rectum were removed and the surgeon fashioned a false rectum out of the bottom of my ileum. Sadly that pouch has been ulcerated ever since. The more stressed I get, the more often I have to go to the loo. I was getting up four or five times a night with the stress.

Throughout all the time till I was ordered out of my house by a judge, Charlie was kept away from me, except when there was some petty spiteful motive to disrupt something I had planned to do. Even the contact periods ordered by the court were regularly broken and abused. Over the years it became increasingly frustrating that the judges simply refused to deal with the problem practically. Emma being an intelligent and gutsy person realised early on that there was a strong prejudice in her favour. Unsurprisingly she went on to wreck contact order after contact order with impunity.

Emma often interfered with my contact time by remaining in the room and keeping up a quiet stream of verbal abuse. This put me on edge and Charlie would pick up on this and not interact so readily. Other common disruptions were arriving with Charlie ten minutes late and taking Charlie away fifteen minutes early in the hour long contact sessions. Sometimes Emma would claim that Charlie was asleep in the yoghurt room. No other time would be suitable. So when I did get Charlie and the weather was nice I attempted to take Charlie outside for a walk or to see the animals. This resulted in the disappearance of his coat and boots before contact times. The frustrating thing was that there was no one to referee these problems. I would complain to my solicitor and we would log all the contact disruptions. When she felt we had logged enough she would apply to the court to complain. This process would take two to three months, sometimes longer. In court Emma would deny the allegations, then she would invent all sorts of excuses, and if the judge seemed bothered by her actions (invariably they were not) she would agree to improve in future. Later on as Charlie got older a similar pattern evolved, denial of breaking the order, excuses and then apparent contrition. When a new order was given she would comply for a few months, then break it completely knowing it would take three to four months to get the matter back into court. The police, I found, have a very biased role. If Emma contravened the order as the resident parent (the parent seen as looking after the child for the majority of the time) the police would not get involved. It was a civil matter and had to dealt with by the court. If I did anything contravening the contact order, however, they were quick to threaten me with arrest.

When the hearing to deal with the breaches from the first order came around, I was dumbfounded to see the judge acknowledge that there had been significant breaches, but not once admonish Emma for her behaviour. Emma demanded that I not drive Charlie in a vehicle as, she alleged, I was a dangerous driver. The judge imposed that restriction on me, without any supportive evidence being produced. Emma also got the judge to agree to an all day nursery placement for Charlie, two days a week. I objected as this was clearly a move designed purely to keep Charlie away from me, and meant that I had less contact time. At 17 months of age, I thought he was too young for all day nursery. The judge would not allow an interim hearing to discuss this. He then asked if violence would be a consideration in the judgement. Emma's solicitor suddenly announced it was. He went on to say that as I was cruel to animals, I was a danger to Charlie they claimed, supposedly supported by some American research that correlated cruelty to animals would lead on to cruelty to children. My barrister and I were incredulous. The judge gave Emma's legal team (amazingly on legal aid) 21 days to submit allegations and witness statements. I asked my solicitor if we could appeal to the high court for an interim hearing. I was repeatedly told I would be wasting my money.

Early in the New Year I was served with a summons by a court bailiff. Emma brought an injunction against me for a hearing on the 10th. She was applying to have me evicted from the farmhouse and for a non-molestation order to be imposed. There was a hearing already booked for contact review a few days later. With injunctions there is little time for preparation or to react. Emma had removed the fax machine and phone to the yoghurt room on our farm. I needed to send some statements to my solicitor quickly, so I asked for the fax machine to be moved back into the kitchen. Emma ignored my request so later in the day I brought it over. Emma tried to physically prevent me, but I pushed her out of the way. I installed it in the kitchen. I was also awaiting a response by fax. I then had Charlie for contact. When that had finished I discovered that the fax machine had been sabotaged.

The hearing when it came turned out to be largely procedural. Emma's cross petition for unreasonable behaviour was ruled out of time but the judge did allow Emma to refute my allegations in each hearing. He gave timescales for answers to the questions for the first Ancillary Relief hearing (financial matters) to be filed. I was served in court with another summons, this time to have me evicted from my company. The judge ruled it would all be heard just a couple of days later. So instead of 14 days to build a defence I had a day and a half. The thrust of Emma's allegations was that I had interfered with the staff so they had left. I was really angry at my legal team for first not foreseeing such tactics, and secondly not suggesting a similar non-molestation order against Emma months before. So I rushed around contacting staff that I knew and explained what had happened. Two of them wrote short letters for the court; the others said they did not want to get involved. Greg, the stockman, I knew was already in league with Emma over the divorce.

Predictably as she did after most hearings Emma became more obnoxious and contact with Charlie was withdrawn. When we went back to court we asked for an adjournment. I had to sign undertakings. Emma refused to sign cross-undertakings. I was banned from entering the yoghurt building, farm buildings and interfering with the business or management.

At another child matters hearing in March we were before a district judge I had nicknamed the dinosaur. He was a ponderously slow, pompous man. One of his first statements before us was to tell us that he liked to crack the tough nuts. He would soon sort us out. It was a contact hearing but part way through he suddenly blurted out to my barrister that there was no way I would ever get joint residency (custody). The subject of residency was not being discussed. The judge was completely out of order. After objecting three times to his comment we were threatened with eviction from the courtroom. My barrister and I both made formal complaints about his behaviour, but neither of us had a reply or answer to those complaints. We had a back-to-back hearing for the divorce finances but the judge became noticeably biased after our heated exchanges. My barrister wanted to appeal, but I did not want to delay the divorce process over a relatively small matter. The most recent court order also enabled me to put Charlie to bed one night a week. This was an action too far for Emma. She sabotaged every attempt and disgracefully used Charlie to make the process difficult. At the times that Emma invaded our contact time I did not stop Charlie from going to her or being hugged by her. I always put Charlie first even though at times I wanted to yell and scream at Emma. Emma was ruthless in using Charlie to get at me.

A theme developed over the next few years: I was accused of all the things that Emma actually did to me. My therapist assured me that it was her way of addressing her guilt by putting it all on me. But in a court of law it was her word against mine. In our Family law courts I was to learn the hard way that the judges automatically favour motherhood unless there is strong irrefutable evidence to the contrary. In my case, as in most divorces, there were no witnesses to these family situations. Indeed whenever there were other people around Emma made sure she behaved. It took a process of years with opinions from professionals involved with the case to change the perception of the judges. What annoyed me so much was that there emerged a clear pattern, but the prejudice of the judges still gave her the benefit of the doubt time and again, even after seven years. Emma had supporters who were prepared to lie in court too. Some like Greg, the stockman, were just opportunists expecting some pay off, but most like neighbours and her relatives were simply told fabricated stories about me and my behaviour. Often I overheard Emma talking on the phone to supporters giving a completely spun account of an incident. I kept thinking that she would revert back to the upright, moral, honest person that I had fallen in love with. I just could not believe that she would do to Charlie what her mother had done to her. It took me, stupid me, about four years for the penny to drop that I was her number one enemy and that she would never change. She would do anything it took to keep me from being in Charlie's life, irrespective of the effect that had on our son!

After negotiations at an ancillary relief hearing, the final directions hearing, the judge ordered certain information to be ready for the final hearing. There was a child matters hearing, back to back. The judge ordered CAFCASS to investigate my allegations of Emma's behaviour and treatment of Charlie, and the emotional abuse. Emma's barrister suddenly announced that they wanted an emergency hearing to have me evicted from the farmhouse. The judge also ordered a new contact order. My barrister was concerned that Emma would provoke me to violence as the harassment continued. He emphasised that any violence would destroy our case at a stroke. We were told that the emergency hearing would be in four days. When I got home I packed my bags and went to stay with my uncle.

My aunt and uncle were a tower of support and understanding. It was odd that of all my siblings I had had the least contact with them, but they welcomed me with open arms. Uncle Jim was very generous and gave me £5,000 to start my legal fight, when I had no funds available. I also used their local family law solicitor firm. It was all a steep learning curve for me: the whole legal experience. I took the naïve view that as I was paying large amounts of money for the advice, it must be good. But my solicitor had never dealt with an opponent of my wife's calibre. She would often exclaim that Emma could not do such and such only for Emma to do just that; she had never dealt with someone who paid little or no attention to orders, directives or deadlines or simply refused to answer questions. We would regularly be given important documents just as we arrived at court, instead of the customary days before. Emma changed her solicitor many times. I like to think the more ethical amongst them would not go along with her tactics. I know one of them refused to act anymore until they got paid.

The emergency hearing was a disaster. We went before a circuit court judge in court number 13. Emma gave evidence first, then me, then Greg. The judge was a very pompous man. He upbraided anyone who pronounced words like harassment the American way. To his credit he did not like waffle. My barrister lost the plot twice, while he was cross-examining Emma and Greg. He was a very poor speaker and waffled a lot. He plainly irritated the judge. Later the judge cracked a joke in poor taste, there were muted titters around the court. My barrister proceeded to criticise the judge for his poor joke, on and on. I cringed as he dug a bigger and bigger hole for us. Eventually the judge came to his summing up. He started by saying that he had to make a decision, but he did not know which account of events to believe, Emma's or mine. He said he decided on Emma's for a list of reasons, largely it seemed because Greg backed up many of her stories, supposedly as a witness. For example Greg said he had witnessed me deliberately run over Emma with the car—at the time of that incident, which certainly did not involve me running over Emma, he was in the barn dealing with the goats over 200 yards away! Apparently he had seen me cutting electric fencing, leaving gates open and interfering with the milking parlour. On top of that I had apparently also harassed the staff.

We were gearing up for a final hearing for child matters and contact. My solicitor said she had never seen or heard of a statement like that produced by Emma about the cruelty to animals she had brought up earlier. Emma was also going for an interim hearing to reduce my contact time. She claimed that Charlie was showing disturbing behaviour. Charlie, aged 3, was allegedly masturbating and spreading excreta around the house. He would apparently be in a 'manic state' after contact. The court hearing was on September 19th. In the run up to the hearing, contact was denied because Charlie had a cold. One contact was halved but I saw no sign that Charlie had a cold.

At the court there were 8 other cases before the judge that day. We went before the judge last thing before lunch and then back after lunch for a little more than the half hour pencilled in for our case. The judge would not consider staying contact (overnight). I suggested that Emma and Charlie move into the house Charlie had inherited from his grandmother, two miles from the farm. I could then move back into the farmhouse to make contact easier. Emma vetoed this. The judge allowed Emma to swap the Saturday contact with Friday so she could have weekends with Charlie, unless or until I had a job that conflicted. He ordered psychological assessments of Emma and I, and CAFCASS to report on contact for a final hearing.

A contact and child matters hearing was due which was to be followed by the final finance hearing. A trial in the Magistrates court, the result of an arrest for a trumped up charge of 'domestic violence' against Emma, was also set. Emma tried to postpone the contact hearing till after the magistrate's court date. We turned up for a pre-trial review hearing before a district judge who had a terrible stammer. He agreed that the contact issue needed d-d-d-discussing and ordered the contact hearing to go ahead. The guardian had spoken to Emma after the arrest and without talking to me, wrote to the court asking for the hearing to be postponed and added that his report was now out of date following the arrest. It seemed I was judged guilty of assault before my trial. We met Emma's new solicitor, who was extremely prickly and aggressive. Over the years ahead my barrister and other solicitors would complain that she was an extension of Emma. She usually refused to talk in a civilised way and often broke the rules and procedures for document presentation at court. Opposing solicitors often get together to try to find ways forward and to try to solve problems: not this woman! All my legal team complained that she was always obstructive. Often I laughed that Emma had finally found someone like her, who would do her bidding. In fact one of my solicitors got so frustrated with her attitude that he investigated her legal background. With great indignation he claimed she was not even a fully qualified solicitor. At the next hearing we were before a lady judge again. After heated argument contact was reinstated again but I was not allowed to go to the farm again for exchange. Apparently Emma was too frightened. So it was agreed to use the nursery school for exchange. The guardian did not appear, but he was ordered to redo his report and organise a psychologist to assess us and report to the court.

Before the final finance hearing Emma came up with a series of last minute offers for settlement. I wanted the judge to decide. My solicitor came to the final hearing with my ancillary relief barrister. She had always said there was no point in her going with my child matters barrister as it was just duplicating my costs unnecessarily. She actually did a lot of the drafting of the final agreement and gave lots of good advice on the day during the negotiations. When we arrived at court the negotiations started. If a negotiated settlement can be made, then it goes before the judge to rubber stamp it. If no agreement is reached the judge imposes what he thinks is fair. Just before the hearing Emma had changed her position. She now demanded to keep the farm and business to provide her with an income. I was sure she did not want to farm, and pointed out that the processing business could be operated from an industrial estate locally. The farm had been valued at a ridiculously low amount in my opinion. A few years before the separation we had built a new yoghurt building at a cost of £70,000. It had been designed to be converted into two holiday cottages when we retired from the dairy business. The valuer refused to put a value on it. Yet later on Emma was to rent this ‘valueless’ building out for £150 per week. Stupidly I had agreed to the valuation as the arguments over it had already accrued a bill with the solicitors for over a thousand pounds. As we had agreed to sell the farm I thought the valuation was fairly academic. Now Emma had changed her demands I was outsmarted.

My barrister spoke to the usher to tell him that negotiation had not been successful so we were ready to go before the judge. Miraculously the opposition's offers improved from a start point of £80,000 for me and maintenance for Emma to £195,000 with a clean break settlement. A clean break settlement meant I was not liable to pay any maintenance for Emma thereafter. My bottom line was 49% of the valued assets (less a range of costs) at £200,000. Eventually I was able to present this in an acceptable approach to which Emma could agree. Then we moved on to the possessions. Emma refused many items on my list. I refused to budge, to the point where my own barrister was pleading with me to give way as she saw the whole agreement coming apart. I stuck to my guns, and when the usher informed us that the judge had dealt with the other cases before him and wanted to hear our case, Emma agreed to sign. It took some time to draft the agreement before the judge signed it off. I simply asked for all my possessions before the marriage to be returned and one painting by a relative, given as a wedding present. I made no claim on the other wedding presents or any of her possessions inherited from her father. There were a few small items from a selection that we had bought together that I asked to keep, along with all my birthday presents given to me during the marriage. Unfortunately I was never to see many of them. I did not ask for either of our dogs as I did not want them split up. Sadly when the order was transcribed by the court the first sentence was omitted. We did not spot the error till we tried to enforce the order. I had no idea how difficult enforcing it would turn out to be. A lot of effort had been put into the wording of the settlement so that Emma could not wriggle out of it, especially the default arrangements for the financial settlement.

I appeared at the Magistrate's Court for the trial of the assault charge. I was introduced to a young friendly counsel, who disappeared to discuss the case with the Crown Prosecutor. He opined that the case should have been dealt with in the civil courts. He also suggested that rather than go to trial, I should be bound over to keep the peace. My counsel took me to one side to explain this. The prosecutor took a long time to persuade Emma not to go to trial. There was another trial being heard before our case. Eventually Emma agreed. I was ushered into the dock and the panel of three magistrates came in. The chairman was my retired homoeopathic veterinary surgeon. When he saw me he left the room immediately. There was much whispering and it was explained to me that he could not sit in judgement of me if he knew me. So I was transferred to court number 2 when it became available. I stood in the dock as the lady magistrate read out and explained about being bound over to keep the peace. She then dismissed the case. Bail conditions were lifted and if I kept the peace there would be no conviction. I went to say goodbye to my counsel. The Crown Prosecutor happened by and came over to thank me for my honest statement and remarked that he was irritated that the matter had come to court, a waste of everyone's time. We all shook hands and I left.

After one very difficult time when an incident with Charlie was blown out of all proportion, Emma applied to court to vary the order. She had changed her approach and now laid allegations of mental and physical abuse of both her and Charlie. She also produced a medical report from the local hospital hoping to imply sexual abuse of Charlie too. The report specifically said there was no evidence to suspect sexual abuse. The only reason to produce the report was to smear me and introduce further doubt in the judge's mind.

I was livid that Emma had put Charlie through such an ordeal and the inevitable questions that then arose about daddy. Mud usually sticks! My barrister was angry that the judge did not reprimand Emma and her legal team for such reprehensible behaviour. Emma then produced a schedule of Charlie's supposed problems sleeping and difficult behaviour after each contact. This formed the basis of her demand to stop staying contact and reduce contact to a couple of hours at a time. For the first time I began to seriously worry about how low Emma would stoop in her fight to stop me seeing Charlie. The barristers tried to do a deal before going before the judge, but I refused to reduce my contact time or give up staying contact. The judge refused to substantially change contact. He wanted the first two consecutive Saturdays to be day contact to reintroduce Charlie to me. He was taken aback by Emma's furious fight not to share the travelling by picking up Charlie from my house. The judge also gave me dates to have Charlie over the coming Christmas. Both barristers requested that a Circuit or High Court judge hear the case in future. The judge granted my request that Greg the stockman be ordered not to be present at future exchanges. Charlie's nursery teacher had written to the court to say that Charlie had no behavioural problems when he was handed back to her after contact. When Emma heard that she refused to allow exchanges there in future.

One afternoon before contact my solicitor rang me to tell me that Emma had refused all further contact for the time being. This was to allow Charlie to have some counselling in peace to overcome the trauma of contact with me. My new solicitor made an "ex-parte" application to attach a penal notice to the last order for Christmas contact. He managed to get an emergency hearing; the last slot on December 23rd before the court closed for the holiday. My barrister could not attend, so my solicitor made the application before the circuit judge. Emma's barrister, who had a very bombastic and aggressive style, was reprimanded by the judge for trying to delay the proceedings on a technicality. The judge told us to go in recess and sort out the Christmas dates between us. Emma still refused contact so we went back before the judge. The judge explained that he expected an order to be obeyed, otherwise some sanction would be applied, even to the extent of moving Charlie to live with me. We then had one of the funniest and most surreal moments that I was to experience in court. The judge then asked Emma's barrister to ask Emma if she had understood and would obey the court order. The man stood wringing his hands looking very uncomfortable and replied that his client understood but had instructed him to say she would not obey. The judge was completely taken aback. He repeated the question, adding that he thought she did not understand the gravity of the situation. The hapless barrister again asked Emma; she again responded negatively. Now looking even more uncomfortable, in a very quiet voice the barrister again relayed a negative response to the judge. The judge told Emma to stand up, and he addressed her directly. He explained again and at length the consequences of disobeying a court order, and of being in contempt of court. Emma replied in a level and calm voice that she would not obey the order. The judge was visibly shaken. My solicitor and I had trouble containing our mirth. After a minute or two of silence the judge closed his file, and declared that he would not, at this stage, attach a penal notice to the order as he expected the order to be obeyed. He ordered us all back before him in January to review the situation. My solicitor insisted that I drove down to the farm to collect Charlie for contact just after Christmas on the 27th with a witness to corroborate whether or not Charlie was made available for contact. I was not impressed with my new solicitor's performance in court. He was a poor speaker and seemed unable to recall facts when required. But at least the hearing had been entertaining.

Back before a judge in January, he made no comment on the lack of contact or contempt of court other than to acknowledge it happened. Emma again indicated she would not obey the order. The judge adjourned the case to be heard by the circuit judge. He announced that there was a convention at the courts that if a penal notice was necessary a circuit or more senior judge should attach it. The order for contact was to stand. Later the judge discovered that the earliest opportunity for a suitably senior judge to hear the case would not come up until some 5 months later. He sent a note to all parties stating that the period without contact would be damaging so he was making a hearing date to bring the matter back to court a month later. At that hearing Emma still said she would not obey the order. She wanted contact to go back to being restricted to a contact centre. (Back to square one—a venue designed for father's proven to be a danger to their child.) After much discussion the judge ruled that the order was to stand with some minor adjustments. As Emma indicated that she would not obey, a penal notice was attached to the order including a clause that Greg should not be present at the handovers. Contact was delayed as I had a holiday booked. A District judge could break convention! The judge had applied pressure in his pre-Christmas hearing for us to try mediation again so we had a meeting with a mediator. Emma spoke first and refused to talk about her family background. Most of the time she revisited the history between her and I and wanted to get off her chest all the things that upset her. The mediator was unable to control or direct the topics. When my turn came to speak, Emma picked up her bag and left. The mediator was a bit non-plussed and said she would report that mediation was not appropriate.

I went down to pick up Charlie several times after the February hearing, only to find no one at the farm. After this became a pattern, my solicitor wrote to the judge to ask if I had to continue to waste my time going for contact, only to find Charlie unavailable. The judge agreed I did not have to waste my time with further fruitless journeys. Emma appealed against an earlier order for contact, on the grounds that the judge had not understood the danger that Charlie had been in from me; and had not taken into sufficient account the distress the contact had on herself, not permitting her to have the support of Greg at handovers; nor the effect her emotional breakdown, over contact, was having on Charlie. She lost the appeal, and he found her in contempt of court (for not obeying the contact order).

My solicitor then made an application for committal proceedings, to send Emma to prison. A circuit judge heard this. In his order he upgraded the CAFCASS officer to the position of Charlie's court appointed Guardian and authorised legal representation for Charlie on legal aid. To save me making wasted journeys he ordered Emma to notify me more than 72 hours in advance of contact if Charlie was to be made available. The contact order would remain. Crucially the judge adjourned any consideration of penalty for the contempt of court. Unbelievably Emma was not even reprimanded.

Needless to say I continued to be denied access to Charlie so we went before the court again. On the second occasion before this judge he had looked me in the eye and declared that he would deal robustly with the case and he assured me that he would not just duplicate the excellent work of the District judge, he would make real headway. Sadly he went on to waste everyone's time and money for two years by passing the buck or sitting on the fence till he was forced to send the case up to the High Court. He continually adjourned the decision for a penalty for the contempt of court. Similarly he continuously adjourned any decisions on costs being awarded against Emma. It infuriated me that we had hearing after hearing, which cost £3,000 a time where he could have either forced Emma to comply or move the residency to me and instead he did precisely nothing. At the same time the Cafcass Guardian was equally unwilling to meet his responsibilities. He started from the position of fairly blatant support for Emma over the false assault charge. After a few hearings I became quite wary of him as he would say things to me privately, but then in court would take an opposite view. As a man he was easy to get on with, and easy to talk to but over the years I realised he had little backbone and avoided making any decisions if he could. Indeed at one hearing he leant over to tell me that the judge wanted him to make the decision for him. The Guardian was determined not to make any decisions for the judge, he barely made them for himself! Over the years in his reports he put forward the ideal result for Charlie. We all agreed it, but given Emma's attitude to contact this was increasingly proving not to be a practical option. He went on right up to the end advocating contact as 'the answer' even when contact was impossible to maintain. Towards the end of his participation in the case, on leaving the court hearings, he would comment that the contact arrangements ordered by the judge would not work. Yet he had pushed for those arrangements, against everyone else. As things got more difficult he eventually admitted to being intimidated by Emma.

When Emma next gave evidence she assured the judge that she had seen the light, and was now converted to the benefits of re-establishing a meaningful relationship between Charlie and I. It was just what the judge and the Guardian wanted to hear. I did not believe a word of it. Emma agreed to start therapy with someone approved by the expert, and to implement the contact plan. The judge ordered us back for a review at a later date. By this time I had not seen Charlie for 15 months. Emma had successfully delayed everything by pure brinkmanship with the judges. When the mood of the court changed to seriously consider the issue of a change of residence, Emma affected a miraculous U turn in court. The judge grasped at that particular straw and adjourned all outstanding issues of costs and the penalty for contempt of court.

The next hearings were arranged for a detailed discussion of the therapy Emma was supposed be to undergoing and on how progress with contact was being made. Emma delayed the start of therapy to such an extent that we eventually had to get an emergency hearing to highlight the problem. But, on the other hand, contact was progressing as envisaged and going well. Finally Emma saw her therapist for the first time just before the next hearing, giving no chance for a report on progress to be made.

Then came a hearing for Emma to challenge the CAFCASS Guardian. She accused the guardian of not protecting Charlie from me, nor considering what was in Charlie's best interests and of failing to research matters fully. On the face of it, it was an extraordinary tactical error. The guardian, when in court, consistently supported her position as primary carer and acquiesced to many of her demands over contact. He bent over backwards time and again to give her the benefit of the doubt and another chance, much to my legal team's disgust. But she had now declared her position and openly distanced herself from the guardian as she had undermined his work with Charlie. She had gauged him as a weak man who could be prevented from doing his job properly if she intimidated him. She had prevented him from seeing Charlie for the last two years of his involvement and successfully prevented him from visiting Charlie's schools and talking to his teachers. An application to replace the guardian had been dismissed as the judge said he was a Cafcass officer of enormous experience and was one of the most senior officers in the district. He went on to say that over the years he had been involved in cases with this guardian he had developed an enormous respect for his work. For my part I entirely agreed with Emma that the guardian was pretty useless, but I remained silent, as it was also obvious that had she been successful in having the guardian replaced, the whole court process would have been delayed for months. Any replacement would have had to spend time meeting all the parties, especially Charlie.

Although contact had increased and improved Emma began to become more and more difficult. She was particularly angry at the proposition of the two 5 day contacts. There was a barrage of abuse for both my partner Karen and I with accusations that we were undermining Emma's relationship with Charlie. There were constant allegations of inappropriate things being said to Charlie, such as apparently telling him that Emma was not his mother.

We reached the final hearing and over the three days an expert explained at length what she thought lay behind Charlie's refusal to go on contact. As the plan for increasing contact was implemented

Emma became more and more angry at the rebuilding of the relationship between father and son. The further prospect of longer contact periods, up to 7 nights at Christmas, had made Emma more and more anxious. As Charlie was a single child living with, to all intents and purposes, a single parent he was very responsive to his mother's moods and especially to her anxiety. Charlie, within the context of the two parental relationships, was desperate to please both his mother and father. But his bond with his mother was considerably stronger. So to reduce the tensions at home he placated his mother by refusing to go on contact.

There was no more contact before the next hearing, but out of the blue, Charlie rang me by himself. He was whispering and explained that his mother was out. Even so he was very worried that mother would find out. The second time he said he was hiding under the bed. In court Emma had said she had put my phone number on the calendar in the kitchen, and she had encouraged Charlie to ring. Whatever was true it was apparent that Charlie wanted to speak to me but without his mother's knowledge. He was in turmoil.

Experts produced yet more reports and one of the experts was ordered to see Emma to assess the impact of the therapy. Emma refused and the report was one page long in the form of a short letter in which Emma's therapy was described as having made good progress. There was no detail in the report. At the hearing the judge accepted that little assessment of the effect of the therapy on Emma has been produced. The expert psychologist commented that Emma's statement before the court, continued to show that she believed her "attitudes, beliefs and behaviours were appropriate and that she was protecting her son from harmful emotional stress by refusing contact. She did not appear to be fully open towards the idea that there may be benefits to Charlie through being in a harmonious relationship with both parents." The judge and guardian were made aware of another expert having written that Charlie should not be allowed to come to me for Christmas for fear of 'emotional damage' as set out in a letter from Emma's solicitor. As well as the application to remove the guardian again there were efforts to sort the Christmas contact between the parties. In his summation at the January hearing, the judge said that this comment had influenced the guardian's recommendation to cancel the Christmas contact. The judge explained that he had declined to address the matter in court as there was not enough time. He was critical of remits being exceeded and attempts to influence the courts in that way. This was an example of what I call the underhand and disreputable tactics by Emma's solicitors. They introduce something that shouldn't have been introduced, knowing the impact it would have on some parties to the proceedings. They would then make a simple apology to the court, but by then the damage was done.

On one occasion the judge was so angered by their disregard for procedures that he applied a financial penalty on her solicitors. Before the expert psychologist was finally approved to report on Emma, a "tame" psychologist assessed her. A report was written and Emma's legal team tried to have it introduced instead of the court appointed experts. At the time the judge was so angry he left the court for several minutes.

At the next three-day hearing the presiding judge realised there was not enough time to cover everything. He adjourned matters to be completed later. He made a detailed, lengthy judgement; about 25 pages of transcript. He ordered that no further sanctions be imposed for the contempt of court (outstanding) and no cost orders were to be imposed with the exception that Emma had to pay the costs of the failed appeal hearing. Full residence was granted to Emma. Emma was to make Charlie available for contact as arranged by the guardian. The parents and the guardian were to identify a family therapist for joint therapy to assist in longer-term support for contact.

One of Emma's main arguments at the hearing was that her anxiety was incredibly heightened by not having formal legal residency of Charlie. The constant threat that Charlie could be moved, she maintained, made the situation intolerable for her and Charlie. It was our argument that this stick was the only effective method of getting Emma to comply with contact and other issues. The judge said that he now accepted that Emma had completely reversed her views on contact and was going to support contact and the relationship between Charlie and I. In order to facilitate this and to remove the extra uncertainty he granted her the legal residency of Charlie. She assured the court that she would restart contact quickly. The guardian was ordered to explain the judgement to Charlie in simple terms at school, organise the resumption of contact, and to organise the selection of the therapist. He failed to do the first two points.

Given the history of the case and Emma's consistent implacable hostility, it was hard to believe the judge was so naïve as to believe that Emma had, for the second time, and in order to get what she wanted, suddenly, apparently, accepted all the benefits that contact with me would have for Charlie.

Prior to an earlier hearing I had explained to the guardian that my relationship with Karen Brown was coming adrift; probably as a result of all the stress I was experiencing. Since moving into her new house I had experienced a level of control from Karen that severely tested my concept of trust. I experienced echoes of the problems I had had with Emma. I decided to leave. Karen, however remains very supportive and my closest friend. She encouraged me to stay till after the January hearing to lessen the stress that moving would entail if I moved out beforehand. The guardian informed the court of my change in circumstances. I found a flat to rent in the next village.

I saw Charlie for a short day contact after the hearing. The handovers took place at a local shopping village. We spent the time at my sister Laura's house and I gave Charlie all his Christmas presents.

At the last hearing the guardian had commented on behavioural problems Charlie was having at school. I applied to his school for all the reports they had sent to the guardian. I was surprised to find reports of bad behaviour going back to 2005, especially it seemed after the visits to see the guardian at his office. I had had no contact with Charlie for the whole of 2005 and early 2006. Charlie was reported to be talking about "that bad man" meaning the guardian. He was also telling teachers about a bad daddy trying to take him away from mummy. During counselling he expressed his worry that a judge might not let him live with his mother anymore. He described quite a knowledge of the court process. Emma refused to allow any further counselling sessions privately for Charlie as Emma claimed the counsellor was no longer impartial. The expert had observed that Emma reacted very aggressively to any professional who tried to establish an independent working relationship with Charlie. In the end Emma took Charlie away from the school and enrolled him in another junior school. She claimed the reason was because Charlie was being bullied. This was strenuously denied by the school. It was a pattern I had seen often with professionals that Emma perceived as against her or critical of her.

After a total of four days plus a day of final submissions and the judgement, the result was that my relationship with Charlie was considerably worse and the future was uncertain. All the judges, over the years had emphasised how important the court saw it that father and son have a good relationship, and that the court would do everything in its power to promote this. Where there was continual obstruction the court could and would consider moving the child to the non-resident parent. After 5 years of continuous obstruction however, no sanction was ever brought to bear on Emma. The best period of contact had only been achieved after the threat of a penal notice and the threat that non-compliance could result in Charlie moving to live with me. Twice Emma had promised in court that she had had a 'conversion' and would promote and support Charlie in having a proper relationship with his father. My legal team were disgusted at the outcome and foresaw continued problems over contact. In fact my barrister said that for the first time in his career he was ashamed of the profession he worked in. Earlier my barrister had asked permission to send the case up to the High Court. At that time the judge had said he was perfectly capable of dealing with the matter and refused permission.

For the judge to refuse to punish Emma for the outstanding contempt of court or award any costs against her for the endless hearings that had been necessary, at great cost in time and money, to deal with her bad behaviour, was extraordinary. Giving Emma all that she demanded from the court was tantamount to giving her the green light to carry on as before. She was rewarded for her appalling behaviour. At the time I said I did not know if the judge's actions were incompetence, prejudice or just bias. We discussed appealing to the High Court. My barrister was prepared to appeal but thought the chance of success would be low as the appeal judge would most likely rule that his colleague was entitled to view the matter as he did. A more senior judge would be loath to overturn a judgement without strong cause, I was told.

I was getting more and more angry and frustrated at the lack of progress towards having contact with Charlie. It was blatantly obvious to me that yet again Emma had lied in court about her conversion. I also felt the judge had as usual grasped the easy option and acquiesced to all her demands. He then put the control of the progress back to contact in the guardian's hands, whom I knew to be no match for Emma. The guardian came to see me at my flat. He surprised me again by actively encouraging me to seek change in residence. As, as far as I could see that was no longer on the agenda for the foreseeable future I had taken a flat where the landlord expressly forbade resident children. It was alright for weekend visits but not full time occupancy. So I explained that I would have to move. Luckily there was a six-month break clause in the tenancy agreement. At the end of July I moved to a three-bedroom house with a garden and garage in a village. I also considered what kind of job I could do if Charlie came to live with me. My agency driving work fluctuated a lot. Renting a house also meant I had to live off my savings as well. Rent and council tax was around £1000 a month, whilst my agency work earned me about £800 a month after deductions and Charlie's maintenance. Sometimes there were weeks with no work. I tried to get weekend work and night shifts as the rates were much better. I decided to train as a driving instructor as this would give me flexibility if Charlie came to live with me. Once again I was putting my trust in the courts to do the right thing.

By this time I was writing letters direct to Charlie, but I had no way of knowing whether or not he was receiving them. I was not allowed to ring Charlie and Charlie no longer rang me. It later transpired in court later that my phone number had been put on the December calendar but that when that was replaced by the January calendar, my phone number was not replaced.

Emma demanded that I comply with the financial settlement order and send her the TR1, which would transfer of ownership of the deeds of the property to her. I refused as she still owed the outstanding interest on the late payment for the financial settlement. My solicitor had always advised not to send it until I received the full payment as it was the only leverage I had left. Without the TR1 to enable her to transfer the deeds into her sole name, she was unable to borrow money against the property without my joint signature.

It became apparent that one of her previous firms of solicitors was suing her for non-payment of her legal bill. She needed a loan to pay it. Along with the non-payment of the overdue interest money that she owed, she had to provide proof that the original loan and mortgage had been transferred to her sole liability with the banks. She had not complied with this order from the court. At one hearing this matter was negotiated between the barristers in the waiting rooms. I actually signed the TR1 form with my solicitor there witnessed by Emma's barrister. My solicitor said he would send the document on receipt of the cheque. Emma then promised to send it, along with proof from the banks that liability had been transferred to her sole charge. Unsurprisingly Emma never sent the cheque. She later claimed that a friend had lent her the money to pay the bill. But at every hearing from then on when she was still LIP, she asked the judge to deal with the TR1 issue. It rumbled on and on.

The judge again adjourned the outstanding costs issue from previous hearings but ordered that we were at liberty to apply to have the matter dealt with at another hearing. My solicitor, still engaged just for the costs issue, applied to the court to have it sorted out. As we had come to expect Emma, now LIP, refused to supply any information to enable a hearing to be of any use. Finally we had a hearing back before a District judge to have an oral examination of her finances. She had claimed that she could not pay as she was bankrupt. As she was LIP the judge was very patient and explained everything at length and even gave her advice on what to do if she wanted to contest the costs order. She did her tearful "I can't cope with all the extra stress" act, but the judge would not change the substance of the matter. When we came before the judge who had advised us to make this a separate issue the following month for contact matters, Emma again put on a tearful act about the costs matter. Incredibly the judge then criticised me for pursuing the matter and said it was another reason that things were so difficult between us and that my insistence was impacting on Charlie! Naturally, I was not allowed to speak on the subject. I wanted to say that this issue wouldn't have been a problem if he had dealt with the matter properly two years previously. He ordered a stay on the costs matter, until further notice. In effect he froze the proceedings, letting Emma off the hook yet again.

The guardian reported that the child counsellor had found Emma's manner threatening at times. The guardian and Charlie's solicitors did eventually get a long statement from her in which this counsellor was very critical of Emma and how she dealt with Charlie's emotional needs. For reasons I have never understood, the guardian and Charlie's solicitor did not produce this statement for a full 8 months after it was compiled, missing an earlier trial date.

The guardian wrote an updating letter for the judge. In it he put forward three choices for the court to consider for Charlie:

1) No future contact till Charlie was grown up,
2) Change of residence to the father,
3) Further attempts to arrange contact.

When it came around, the next hearing turned out to be significant. When the judge was informed that the joint therapy had not got past three sessions he was very irritated. He threw his hands up in the air and exclaimed that he could not deal with the case anymore. He sent the case up to the High Court and ordered a directions hearing. At last, a year after requesting that the case be moved to the High Court, he had admitted defeat and let a more senior judge deal with the case. In the two years that he had controlled the case we had not moved on with contact, or from the original judgement. A more detailed assessment had been made of Emma, but overall we had spent an enormous amount of money with nothing to show for it, except an increase in stress levels. The judge further ordered that

Charlie be psychologically assessed and we all had to agree on an expert to assess the likely impact on Charlie of an order for no contact, an order transferring residence to father, or contact orders being made within continuing proceedings.

So another year was lost not seeing Charlie.

During the time I was a Litigant in Person (LIP) (see chapter Litigant in Person and the McKenzie Friend) I had a McKenzie friend Adrian, with me at the first hearing before the more senior judge. He helped me draw up a position statement prior to the hearing. The position statement was drawn up in language that, compared to my barrister's language, was very combative. It was a lot more technical, legal and demanding of the court rather than cooperative. We had to agree an expert child psychologist. Adrian was adamant I had to put forward someone who had experience of dealing with residency change. In his opinion CAFCASS would opt for a pliable psychologist who would deliver the recommendations they wanted. Emma put forward a name that had already been associated with the case, and the judge ruled there was a conflict of interest. When my contender was named, the judge's demeanour changed completely. He became agitated and appeared to be irritated. He looked at Adrian and said he would not allow our choice as with this individual he foresaw endless appeals if that expert was commissioned. I was quite taken aback by the adverse reaction of the judge and it made me a bit wary of Adrian's advice. As the judge made his opening remarks I was immediately impressed when he addressed Emma directly and said that the courts took a very dim view of any parent that prevented the other parent from having a good relationship with their children. He went on to say that courts took the view that a child benefited enormously from having a loving relationship with both parents. He added that in cases of prolonged obstruction to contact he would have no hesitation in changing residency. Naively, I thought it sounded like he might actually get to grips with our case. I felt quite optimistic.

But this was only a directions hearing. The guardian's choice for expert was endorsed, and was to report on the impact of the three choices outlined earlier. An order was made to observe contact between Charlie and I. Emma insisted contact remained chaperoned by her neighbours, and Charlie's counsellor's statement was to be admitted for the next hearing. There was another order permitting me to have indirect contact by post with Charlie, and Emma assured the court that she would make my letters available to Charlie. When the judge first came in to the court he had had only an hour to look at the bundle of documents, but he had not seen any of the position statements. Charlie's solicitor apologised to the judge and then produced copies for him, my one and a half pages, Emma's forty nine pages. The judge retired for only ten minutes to look at them. When he returned he made a passing remark that judges always appreciated brevity. Emma's position statement was actually a collection of statements, letters and reports going all the way back to the beginning including the cruelty to animals charade. There were also letters from neighbours and friends supporting Emma and accusing me of all sorts of extraordinary things to undermine Emma and cause her stress. There was a statement written by her making all sorts of allegations against me, signed by people like Charlie's friends parents, all attesting to Emma's brilliant parenting skills. The first few times I read this rubbish I was amazed at the sheer energy and doggedness Emma displayed in collecting all this paperwork. It also demonstrated just what spin she had put on the facts as she represented them to her support network. If they had known the truth of what Emma actually did they would have been shocked. For me my divorce and battle to see Charlie was private and I only discussed it with close family and Karen.

In order to reduce costs I had asked my solicitor to inform the other parties about ending my status as LIP as close to the May hearing as possible. This would mean that Charlie's solicitor would retain responsibility for the court bundle (documents). So all the statements and documents for the hearing had to be filed through him. There is a fair amount of work involved with preparing the bundle for the judge, sometimes other parties object to certain documents being included, so agreements have to be reached. The bundle then has to be indexed so when in court the judge can give a page number to any document to which he is referring. This is all very time consuming. Needless to say Emma's solicitors had an avalanche of correspondence about the bundle. Charlie's solicitor was publicly funded. But at least my solicitor did not have management of the case, and that saved costs.

When I met my barrister at court we had to wait around for a long time whilst other cases were heard first. I explained to him about my financial struggle with my solicitors over payment that I had won! (See solicitors). He thought it was highly amusing. He explained that the firm had a reputation for negotiating hard with all barristers over their costs. So much so that they routinely billed higher than normal knowing that the firm would cut the bill anyway. He explained that if I kept control of the witness bundle at the court and kept copies of everything from now on, I should have enough to go to another solicitor if I had to without incurring crippling fees for photocopying files.

In his summation the judge had talked at some length about what he called Emma's previous demonising of me to Charlie. He accepted that Emma had now changed, but he emphasised that in order to help Charlie rebuild a relationship with his father his mother had to actively reverse the demonising. He said this would be a major indicator and proof of the change in attitude by the mother. The ball was firmly in Emma's court. He went on to say that he had got an understanding from Emma that there would be no restrictions over my involvement with the school or any other area of my parental responsibility such as Charlie's health. The judge had ordered that Emma and her legal team draw up the order with the agreements and understandings in her words so that she could not, at a later date, claim she did not understand them.

When the judge ordered that the guardian be relegated to the role as keeper of the files, I saw the guardian as a mechanism to register my complaints and objections on the case that could be referred to when, as I believed they would, things went pear-shaped. When Emma had been assessed she waited a year to raise any objections to her report. As it happened the objections and criticisms about the report centred on descriptions of the untidiness of the home and in particular the piles of unwashed clothes, pots and pans and crockery in the kitchen. The substance of the psychological analysis was not challenged. The judge heard the complaints and criticised the personal and unnecessary nature of descriptions of the living conditions at Charlie's home. But he was also critical of Emma for taking over a year to object. With that in mind I wrote several times to the guardian over the next year to voice my anger and frustration at the continued shenanigans used by Emma to frustrate my rebuilding a relationship with Charlie.

At the end of March the hearing to sort out the costs issue from the appeal hearing nearly four years earlier, came to court. Emma had got an adjournment and the County Court managed to confuse the hearing, lodging it as a child matters hearing with the original judge presiding. I had left the case in my solicitor's hands who had instructed a barrister. I did not attend. It turned out that Emma had refused to pay the bill as presented to her; hence the arranged hearing. When the barrister had drawn up a skeleton argument, as previously ordered by the judge, and it was presented to Emma, she suddenly agreed to pay. But she refused to pay the outstanding costs involved in forcing her to pay. This was the third hearing on the matter, in addition to the hours of work done by my solicitor over the years to get her to pay. The judge ordered Emma to pay the outstanding bill plus only £750 for the court costs. He said the costs applied for were wholly disproportionate to the sum being claimed and excessive. He summarily slashed the costs by 80%. The irony was that his past actions were largely to blame for the high costs, together with Emma's continual need to fight everything. Again the judge appeared to be angry that this matter had come back to court to inflame the on-going child matters proceedings. It was he and he alone that kept this festering battle going for four years. If in the normal manner I had financed the recovery of the costs, then I would not have seen any of the £5,400 owed to me. The solicitors and barrister's costs would have been deducted first.

In my experience the courts are a minefield of prejudice and incompetence. As it was this time, the solicitors ended up considerably out of pocket due to a previous arrangement we had made (see solicitors). When I complained about the loss of contacts and other breaches of the orders, I asked the judge responsible to trigger the clause in his order to bring the matter back before him within 7 days. He instructed me to make a C2 application in the normal way. (This takes months). So I applied through the County Court. They muddled the application. The case was referred to one judge but somehow the original terminally delaying judge got involved again. Because of the muddle at the costs hearing this judge instructed me to apply direct to the more senior judge via his Clerk at the Royal Courts of Justice in the Strand in London.

So instead of going back before him within seven days, it was to take three months. The only beneficial side effect was that now Emma knew I had referred the contact problems back to court, she was now back on good behaviour.

After several delays another hearing was arranged before the more senior judge. The judge kept it very informal: just Emma, myself and the guardian in court. I had produced a proper bundle with chronology. Emma and I produced position statements and relevant evidence such as letters for our arguments. The guardian said he had no role so acted merely as an observer.

The judge said he had read the bundle and asked me to explain why I had called for a hearing. I outlined my main points to substantiate my claim that Emma's conversion was a hoax. Every time I spoke Emma interrupted or spoke over me. I had to ask the judge to intervene. The judge asked Emma to respond. Naturally she claimed everything was going brilliantly. But she took the opportunity to go over old history and to whine that I was not paying any maintenance. The judge asked the guardian for his comments. He had none. In my position statement I had made some strong criticisms of both the guardian and the original delaying judge. The guardian had remained aloof in the waiting room before going before the judge. One of my main appeals to the judge was the lack of progress in weaning off the chaperones from my contact meetings with Charlie. It was a year since the 'final hearing' where he had expressed a wish that the chaperones were withdrawn within three months and staying contact re-established within a year. The court expert's plan had called for the withdrawal of the chaperones over the spring or summer. My complaint was that Charlie was set against it because I believed he was not being encouraged to want this and neither was there any evidence of reframing or that Emma had stopped demonising me. I had lost two of the six contacts so far!

The judge closed the bundle and said he was not inclined to deal with the frictions or with Emma's commitment. He was happy that I was having contact, albeit in his words with minor problems. Bizarrely he then ordered that the chaperones be weaned off by early next year and to have a review hearing in the following March. In effect he gave Emma a further six months to keep the chaperones.

After the hearing I informed both Adrian my Mackenzie friend and my solicitor of the outcome. They both wanted to be kept informed of progress. My solicitor's reaction was that I should either appeal, with all the stress that that would entail, or I should consider backing off for a few years till Charlie was older. For a couple of years I had been voicing my worry that this continual battle was undermining Charlie and his schooling. If the man that Emma had produced earlier as her boyfriend had married her, as he claimed he wanted, I would have been happier knowing that there was a reasonable father figure for Charlie. But it was now apparent that everything about her lover and Emma was not what it appeared. Adrian was more interested in the psychology. He thought first that had I been represented the judge would not have been able to take his lazy attitude over the case. Secondly he felt that most judges have big egos and I had made the judge consider he had been completely wrong in his previous judgement. Emma had hoodwinked him. That was an embarrassing viewpoint. So the judge had ignored the evidence, and because I was awed by the court's power I had gone along with it. I was not assertive enough.

Very sadly after another torturous contact I came to the heart-breaking conclusion that there was little point in Charlie seeing me if it caused so much stress for him as he tried to make everyone happy. So I said I would not see him again until he wanted to see me without other people involved. I explained what I had discussed with Charlie to the chaperones and expressed my thanks for their help in trying to make contact successful. I said I was not prepared to continue with what I saw as a cruel programme of contacts. I said the alienation was so bad that seeing me was just exacerbating the problem and that I saw no evidence of it changing. I was not going to see Charlie for the foreseeable future. One of the chaperones then opened up to me and said they had arrived late because Charlie was hysterical and refusing to go on contact. She went on to say that Charlie hated being forced to write cards and letters every three weeks. I replied that I knew there was a problem with the letters as for quite some time they had been reduced to one or two sentences and unsigned. Apparently, I was told, ever since Charlie had come to stay with me for the longer contacts he had become more and more worried about not being returned to his mother and was convinced that I wanted to take him away from his mother forever. I said I found it strange that Emma had not reassured Charlie as I had never once been late back from contact. I said I had done everything I could in good conscience but I was not going to put Charlie through anymore of this cruelty.

The simple truth was that the plan to put Charlie at the heart of decisions about contact just put too much pressure on him. Charlie was desperate to please everyone, but the bond with his mother was far stronger than with me, and given Emma's extreme hostility Charlie was in an impossible position. The other serious flaw was that the 'expert' was completely fooled by Emma's so-called conversion. Because of that flaw nothing was ever going to work. Extraordinarily, Emma claimed to love her son so much but was prepared to put him through so much stress and turmoil to secure sole control over him. And a father, that had done nothing wrong, had to sacrifice his relationship so that Charlie could have some stability and peace in his young life.

I wrote to tell the judge what I had decided about Charlie's contact and the reasons why. I asked him if he had any ideas on the matter. He replied that it was my decision, he did not condone it and if I wanted to do anything about it I should apply to the court in the normal way. I was pretty angry at his response. At the final hearing he had said that if the contact did not work, he had plenty of other things at his disposal and in his armoury. His constant assurances that he would do everything in his power to support Charlie to have a good relationship with both parents were apparently as hollow as his promise to deal with a parent that obstructed contact.

I mulled over what to do for the rest of the summer. I wrote to Charlie regularly but had no way of knowing if he received the letters. I emailed the judge's clerk to say I would attend the hearing scheduled to discuss a way forward.

A week before the hearing I rang the court to check it was still listed. I was assured it was. I went to court for the scheduled hearing only to be told that they had no record of it. I was referred to the listings officer. She told me the court hearing had been cancelled months ago. On further investigation she told me the judge had closed the case and files and had discharged the guardian. I was almost lost for words that no one had thought to inform me. I had always been told that I was the only person, as the applicant in the case, that could close the case or that it would at the very least require my agreement to do so.

I wrote to the judge for an explanation. He replied that as I had ended contact with Charlie there was nothing else the court could do for me. So he had closed the case. My instinct was that as the case was one that the judges really did not want to have to deal with properly, he took the first opportunity to wash his hands of it. I suspect there were no other options in his armoury, other than having to deal harshly with Emma. And that option had been robustly avoided throughout, both by him and his colleagues.

Finally in October I applied to the High Court for a hearing to ask the judge to enforce the order that had enshrined my parental right to be involved with Charlie's schooling and health matters without interference from mother. The senior judge declined to hear the matter and passed it over to a more junior judge, to be heard. I was eventually notified that the hearing would be heard; the letter informing me arriving barely two weeks before the date. At the time there was considerable disruption with heavy snowfalls in the south of England, together with the usual Christmas postal rush. As a consequence I decided not to risk sending a small bundle to the court in the post, but decided instead to take it with me on the day of the hearing.

When I arrived at the county court, I was informed that the courtroom had been damaged by burst pipes. We adjourned to the Magistrate's court, down the road. I asked the Usher if he would take the small bundle for the judge. He declined. When we went before the judge, he declined to take the documents and proceeded to question Emma, after ascertaining from me that this was a single-issue hearing. He questioned Emma as to what problem she had with me knowing the identity of the school. Her repeated answer to questions around this subject was that she had no problem but Charlie was adamant that his father should not be told. She claimed that Charlie had demanded to leave his current school as he could not trust his father not to go to the school again. Emma went on to claim that during the previous year Charlie's behaviour had deteriorated very badly, following allegations of cheating and stealing. The judge asked if Emma always did what Charlie demanded. She said no, but claimed that in this instance Charlie was so adamant that she had to support him. Emma let slip that Charlie was in the court building. The judge was very displeased and explained sternly that Charlie should not be informed of any of the legal process.

Emma had been criticised by nearly every professional involved for including Charlie in the court process. As she claimed she could not explain Charlie's reasons for wishing to exclude his father from his school, the judge decided that Charlie should explain them to me in person. He had a recess to allow time for Charlie to talk to me. It then took 40 minutes to persuade Charlie to even see me. I met Charlie in the company of the chaperone. Charlie would barely look at me, most of the time he looked down at the table. All he would say was that he did not like me and wanted nothing to do with me. He said he did not trust me. He refused to explain why, other than to state that I had hit mummy. So I explained that that was not true and there was no reason not to trust me. I would continue to be informed of Charlie's progress at school. I said that at his age he did not have the wisdom to choose his school, but could complain if he was unhappy at school. I explained it was a parent's duty to monitor the school and endeavour to make sure their child was receiving the best education available. I said that whether he liked it or not I would be fulfilling that role. For about ten minutes we had a difficult one-sided conversation, going round in circles. He was hostile, so I withdrew. The judge reappeared, and was disappointed to learn that Charlie had been unable to express his reasons.

I asked the judge to consider making a statement or ruling over the fact that Emma had broken the order. He refused to address the matter and instead went on to make an order that Emma should write once a month to me informing me of Charlie's progress at school and in life in general, including photographs. He ordered that Emma would supply copies of any school reports edited so that the school identity remained hidden. The application was adjourned till the end of August 2011. I was refused permission to appeal.

I left the court reeling with the realisation that the judges' repeated assurances that they would support and ensure that I would maintain a link with my son was a complete sham. What should have been an open and shut case of breaking a court order was sidestepped time and time again and the judge had gone on to countermand a more senior judge's order as well as what should have been enshrined as my civil right as a parent. This was another case of blatant prejudice. Because I was refused permission to appeal there is now nothing more I can do to seek justice.

My journey through the courts has been a very negative, emotionally and financially draining experience. I hope the account of what happened to me might help others contemplating or going through a similar experience.

Chapter Three

CAFCASS and Child Matters

If any family finds itself in the courts of this land they can expect the going to be far from smooth. If, as in my case, things were difficult and complex, they can expect to find themselves frustrated, severely out of pocket and completely out of patience and hope.

What is the role of CAFCASS? From my experience it would appear to be that of a jobs-worth. In the beginning I had a woman officer who did an accomplished job in producing her reports on time. It was unfortunate that she apparently took early retirement due to ill health. Her replacement, I was told was one of the most senior officers with more than 20 years' experience. Rather naively I assumed that would be good news. He was a likeable, approachable man. For the early years, whilst contact seemed the right way forward, he seemed to be biased towards the mother. I accept and of course agree that for very young children and obviously for those children still on the breast, the child is best with the mother: unless she is a serious threat to the child. As the case progressed and contact became more difficult to support, my concern was not so much his bias toward Emma as his apparent unwillingness to engage and do his job properly. As an official guardian he had considerable powers which he did not appear at all inclined to use. I was very surprised that the judge never questioned him over his inability to see Charlie, as he was supposed to, let alone question and criticise his shortcomings in dealing with the schools and other professionals with whom he was supposed to be liaising. Additionally there appeared to be very little constructive dialogue with Social Services. At some point it was pointed out to me by my barrister that there was a turf war going on over budgets between the two organisations. When I first contacted Social Services months after starting the separation, they refused to get involved as the matter was already before the courts. They seemed not to understand that firstly, in court, you rarely are allowed to speak, and secondly it takes months to get anything before the court. When the school called in Social Services over their concerns for Charlie's behaviour, there appears to have been little inclusion of CAFCASS. Other people complained to Social Services about Emma's behaviour to Charlie, a crucial fact that I only found out from documents before the court. I have swingeing criticism of professional bodies that either through ignorance or incompetence refuse to include the other parent when concerns about children are raised. Many professional bodies refuse to acknowledge parental rights. In fact on two occasions Social Services advised other professionals not to release information about Charlie to me; in direct contravention of the law. I had to get my solicitor to educate them at my expense. I managed to speak to a child psychologist. She recommended that I go to Social Services and accuse Emma of emotional abuse and get the situation investigated. When I contacted Social Services again they said as the matter was before the courts and CAFCASS was involved, they would not get involved. (I later learnt that this was again all about budgets!). It was extremely unfortunate that my legal advisors were not experienced or capable of providing useful advice on the deteriorating situation. But at that stage I was very naïve and "green" myself and had not considered that the expensive advice I was paying for would not be sound.

Early in the proceedings I remember that a CAFCASS officer came to discuss her recommendations for the forthcoming Child Matters hearing with me. She recommended that I look after Charlie when Charlie was not at nursery, and that I should have priority over Emma's mother. I should also have a full day at weekends with Charlie. I was on cloud nine.

At one point Emma cancelled our joint account to which I had no access. This meant that all the direct debits and standing orders I now had to fund myself. She also demanded that I pay for the TV license and the dog food and the personal abuse rose to a peak at the end of January. In court Emma would allege that I treated her in this way or that, but in reality it was what she had done to me! I went to see my MP, to discuss my problems with the legal system. He was dismissive of any suggestion of bias in the courts or from CAFCASS.

It infuriated me that we had hearing after hearing, which cost £3,000 a time where the court could have either forced Emma to comply or move the residency to me. At the same time the CAFCASS Guardian was equally unwilling to meet his responsibilities. He started from a fairly blatant support for Emma over the false assault charge she had made against me. After a few hearings I became quite wary of him as he would say things to me when we would speak privately away from the courts, but then once we got into court he would take an opposite view. All the advisors and professionals connected to the father's support groups like Families Need Fathers made very strong recommendations that I should not in any way cross or unduly upset the CAFCASS case officer: he had, it seemed, the power and position to decide my child's future. His job was to advise the judge as to what was best for the child. There are many horror stories of the consequences of personality clashes between fathers and CAFCASS officers. The Guardian expressed doubts about whether Emma could or would benefit from therapy and apparently had further doubts as to the impact on Emma if residence was changed with regard to whether she would be able to have beneficial contact with Charlie. He wanted contact restarted, and for Emma to undergo appropriate therapy; but added that if this did not work then changing residence should be considered.

Following this there was a hearing for Emma to challenge Charlie's CAFCASS Guardian. She accused the Guardian of not protecting Charlie from me, nor considering what was in Charlie's best interests and failing to research matters fully. On the face of it, it was an extraordinary tactical error: The Guardian, when in court, consistently supported her position as primary carer and agreed to many of her demands over contact. He bent over backwards time and again to give her the benefit of the doubt and chance after chance, much to my legal team's disgust. But she declared her position and so it enabled her to openly distance herself from the Guardian and undermine his work with Charlie. She had identified the Guardian as a weak man who could be prevented from doing his job properly if she intimidated him. She had successfully prevented him from seeing Charlie for the best part of the two years of his involvement and successfully prevented him from visiting the schools that Charlie attended and from talking to the teachers. The judge dismissed the application to replace him by saying that the Guardian was a CAFCASS officer of enormous experience and was one of the most senior officers in the area. Over the years, he informed the court, he had been involved in many cases with the Guardian and had enormous respect for his work. For my part I entirely agreed with Emma that the Guardian was pretty useless, but I remained silent. It was also obvious that had she been successful in having the Guardian replaced, the whole court process would have been delayed for months. Any replacement would have had to spend time meeting all the parties, especially Charlie. The Guardian had only managed to have one meeting with Emma. That meeting was apparently dominated by heated discussion about a letter I had sent to Emma's so called partner. He was usually present when the Guardian saw Emma, and indeed was often at the court hearings to support Emma. Further efforts to have meetings were frustrated by Emma. The Guardian was adamant that contact would not take place unless progress was apparent in the joint therapy, stating that if it was not then contact would have to be supervised to prevent Emma making any further allegations of inappropriate things being said to Charlie by me. He had envisaged supervising some contacts but in reality was unable to organise even his own appointments with Emma. At this time everyone was trying to persuade Emma to continue the counselling that Charlie was having at school. The Guardian asked me to write some letters to Charlie but to send them to him so he could deliver them. I found out later that he never delivered or sent them to Charlie. Nor did he go to the school to explain the judgement to Charlie. He did not see Charlie at all. The Family Assistance Order had a time limit of six months. The Guardian failed abysmally to make use of the extra resources within the time limit.

At one point the Guardian held a professionals' meeting at Charlie's solicitor's office. This was in response to concerns reported by Charlie's school to Social Services. Only Charlie's previous counsellor and solicitor attended. The joint therapist and school supplied written information. Social Services withdrew at the last minute. The meeting concluded that it was appropriate to await the outcome of the joint therapy before considering if any further action was necessary. The Guardian wrote an updating letter for the hearing that had been moved and was to put forward three choices for the court to consider for Charlie:

1) No future contact till Charlie was grown up,
2) Change of residence to the father,
3) Further attempts to arrange contact.

The hearing turned out to be significant. When the judge was informed that the joint therapy had not progressed past three joint sessions he was very irritated. He threw his hands up in the air and exclaimed that he could not deal with the case anymore. He sent the case up to the High Court and ordered a directions hearing. At last a year after requesting that the case be moved to the High Court, the man had admitted defeat and left the way clear for a more senior judge to deal with the case. In the two years that he had controlled the case we had not moved on with contact, nor from the original judgement. A more detailed assessment had been made of Emma, but overall we had spent an enormous amount of money with nothing to show for it, except an increase in stress levels. The judge further ordered that Charlie be psychologically assessed and we all had to agree on an expert to assess the likely impact on Charlie of;

1) An order for no contact.
2) An order transferring residence to be granted and changed to the father.
3) Contact orders being made within continuing proceedings.

So for another year, I had not been able to see Charlie.

In the month before the next hearing I engaged the advice of Adrian Parker from Families Need Fathers. Adrian was often a member of the advisory panel at the Families Need Fathers support group monthly meetings. After one of the summer meetings we retired to a local pub to continue discussions. Adrian explained that he was about to start a business giving advice on contact and residence matters. He was not a solicitor nor was he a lawyer. He had successfully acted for himself in his own divorce. He had also been on lots of legal courses alongside lawyers. He had been acting as a McKenzie Friend for a couple of people. I had brought up the question of continuing or restarting counselling for Charlie at school or privately. The Guardian had reported that the school counselling had finished at Easter and that Charlie's behaviour had deteriorated at school again to such an extent that the school had contacted Social Services. Emma suddenly announced that she had already instructed her GP to set up counselling through CAMHS and that this was to start imminently. After the hearing I contacted the surgery and they confirmed that they had made a referral but Emma never attended with Charlie. Emma's answer to Charlie's problems was to change school in January 2008. And then in early November Social Services got involved again. In her report the social worker stated that anonymous concerns for Charlie's welfare at home had been passed on from the NSPCC. At the same time the school had reported concerns for Charlie at home from comments Charlie had made to teachers at school. The concerns appeared to be about Emma's treatment of Charlie, with Emma frequently screaming and yelling and locking Charlie in his room. The anonymous caller alleged that the mother's behaviour was becoming worse and unpredictable. I was completely in the dark about all of this till I saw the report in documents before the court from the Guardian. Of course Emma accused me of being the anonymous caller to the NSPCC. She and Greg the stockman had fallen out not long before. My guess was that he was either involved or Emma made the call herself in order to label me as being determined to cause her as much trouble as possible. It was not a serious issue for Social Services as they wrote to say that no further action was necessary, case closed.

My barrister objected repeatedly that an assessment by the expert child psychologist based on two contacts and one interview was not sufficient to reach any meaningful conclusion. The expert went on to say that Charlie had indicated that he did want to see his father. There was a certain confidence that the contact could be restarted with Charlie's wishes defining contact. The child psychologist said that Emma had already offered more contacts than the prescribed contact of 4 short contacts with chaperones a year. Part way through this oral testimony, the Guardian's and Charlie's barrister stood up to say that the Guardian withdrew his support for a change of residence because he could not go against the psychologist's professional opinion. He added that he was sceptical of Emma's conversion, given the history of the case. The case sank like a stone.

In his judgement the judge explained that he understood my scepticism of Emma's (third) conversion but agreed with the psychologist that

Emma had apparently had a complete change of heart over contact. On that basis he went on to outline the future of contact, expecting the chaperones to be weaned away from contact in three months.

What is the role of CAFCASS? Is the situation really as bad as my experience suggests? My father would have described the Guardian as a professional civil servant. By that he meant a person who spent much of his time looking after his job rather than doing it. I fail to see how the Guardian could claim to have acted for Charlie in any useful way in the last three years that he was involved with the case. My solicitor and I were baffled by some of his excuses. My biggest criticism of the Guardian was that he failed to stand up for what he privately thought, in court. I always have the greatest respect for anyone who stands by their principles and opinions even if I oppose them. When the Guardian finally expressed his opinion about Emma and Charlie's future in court and in his reports, he retracted them when another professional expressed the opposite view. Rather than do his job and fight for what he thought was best for Charlie, he withdrew his opinion. Indeed he then even tried to resign his role! If I had thought he had genuinely changed his mind I would have accepted that in good grace. However he made it plain shortly after that he still thought the other professional was completely wrong, he had just folded!

So what is the answer and how can the system that is supposed to protect and support children caught in the middle of a court battle actually do that? What I would favour would be a system of mediators with the power of a judge to intervene and have the power to order reports from any experts necessary. These mediators would see the parents for child matters only. There would be no legal representation allowed except for parents with handicapped intellect or poor communication skill. The rough outline would be to allocate a morning or afternoon per family once a month. Initially meetings would be with each parent, then move on to seeing them together. The mediator would stay with the case. A good mediator would get to the bottom of the problems face-to-face fairly quickly. CAFCASS or similar organisations could be engaged to report on schools and housing arrangements etc. These reports could be graded for useful detail and paid for with a reflection of the grade. In the vast majority of cases the problems would be identified within 6 months or 6 sessions. Each session would be recorded and the mediator would keep a file of notes and reports. One of the big problems with the law dealing with family matters is that one size does not fit all. With our open society and different types of parental partnerships case law is often not suitable.

Case law should not apply. At present the law is only changed if a successful appeal is made at the highest level. The judges at the highest level are elderly and generally out of step with modern Britain. In essence the law does not adapt quickly. The government need only to give a broad outline of the basic principles for child matters. The rest is for the mediator and parents to agree. What one couple agrees to does not have to apply to others. The system would do away with legal aid. Orders from the mediator would be written on the spot for each couple, to be shown to police or other agencies as necessary by a parent.

I feel that an urgent shake up of the kind I have mentioned needs to be undertaken. The current legal process is too unwieldy and cumbersome and slows down the agony for all parties involved.

Chapter Four

The Police

The police have a difficult path to tread with domestic violence matters. Often things flare up and then are resolved. If the police were to be too heavy handed this might backfire on them if the warring parties were later reconciled. On the other hand we have all heard horror stories of what happens if they ignore cries for help. During the problems that my wife and I had, the police were called numerous times and on the whole the experience, with a few exceptions, was not too bad. These are some of my recollections of that time.

We had been arguing. Charlie had been put to bed in Emma's bedroom and once she had settled him she came back to have a go at me again. She then went into the storage bedroom (where I had previously slept) and started to throw the large empty boxes into the doorway of the bedroom I was in. I yelled at her repeatedly to stop. I was ignored so I got out of bed. At this point Charlie started screaming, jumping up and down at the barricade Emma had set up in her own bedroom doorway. I went round the barrier, picked him up and cuddled him. Emma became enraged and came bounding out of the second bedroom screaming repeatedly at me to give Charlie to her. I asked her to back off and calm down. She then started to hit and slap me on my shoulder. She was close to becoming hysterical and I realised she was not going to stop. I handed Charlie to her and went to clear the boxes she had thrown into my room. Emma took Charlie downstairs and rang the police. They arrived quite quickly in two cars; I stayed in bed. I could hear lots of laughing downstairs between Emma and the officers who had attended. Eventually I got up and halfway downstairs I was met by a policeman. I asked him how long they intended to stay in our house? There were four policemen. One of them listened to my side of the story and I showed him the scene.

Emma had told the Police that I had two shotguns, which I held legally. They impounded the guns together with Emma's air gun. One of the officers said he would have locked me up too if Emma had not pleaded with them to leave me to milk the livestock, presumably because Greg the stockman was so unreliable now. That was the first of many visits by the Police. At the time what amused me was that Emma, while full of righteous indignation about my firearms, had failed to own up to her possession of an unlicensed .38 Smith and Weston revolver.

I told Emma that as the legal aid board would require accounts to support her request for legal aid I offered to get them up to date. I asked her to clear one of the desks so that I could do that. She refused so I started to clear one of them. She physically tried to stop me. After she repeatedly obstructed me I pushed her to one side. She immediately rang the police. They appeared at 9.30am. One of them, a sergeant, came in to speak to me. He was very helpful and gave me some advice. He said he had been there, done that and got the T-shirt. He told me that I could not win this, that everything was stacked against me. He told me to do the books out of Emma's way, to go somewhere like the library. He also warned me that incidents like this would be used by Emma to fight access. His partner came over to say that Emma felt nervous with me being in the house. They suggested that I leave. So I went to my sister's house for the day.

One thing I soon realised was that if I did anything contravening the contact order, the police were quick to threaten me with arrest. I always remembered what the police sergeant had advised me on his first visit, that there was no way I could win. He made it plain that whatever level of personal abuse I suffered, the police were not interested. What he should have told me was to get in touch with victim support and the local district domestic violence liaison officer and log all the abuse, so they were made aware of the background situation. Later I was to gain some understanding from the district domestic violence liaison officer and eventually an apology for the way the police treated me over the coming months. A typical snapshot recorded in my diary for one awful day in October reads as follows:

I was hoovering the living room carpet when Emma pulled the plug. She said, "What sort of pathetic man allows his wife to stop him working. The doctor, the health worker, the solicitor, everyone plus the police can't believe the way you treat your wife and leave her to run the business and bring up my son without any help!" Emma was even more insufferable than usual. The bullying had slowly increased through the week. I found a note on my door to say I must work on the farm on Monday, and I had to get the frozen milk out to defrost for yoghurt making on Sunday. I told her if she had a problem she had to sort it herself: I no longer worked in the business and would not be working until decent working conditions for me were implemented. She refused my contact with Charlie. Charlie tried to see me himself on Saturday and banged on my bedroom door. Emma took him away twice in floods of tears, saying she could not risk Charlie getting locked in. She went downstairs telling Charlie as usual that I was a nasty, spiteful, sick and dangerous man. On Sunday afternoon Emma said they were going to visit local friends. When I got up to go to the loo at 2am, I found all the lights still on and no sign of Charlie or Emma. In the morning I explained to the staff that I thought Emma had done a runner with Charlie. I put them all on a week's notice that would come into effect unless Emma reappeared within 24 hours. No one was working on the farm so I went down to feed all the livestock. After speaking to my solicitor I rang the police and spoke to the child protection unit. They rang back to say that Emma's solicitor had assured them that Charlie was well and would be returning later that day. I would have my contact later. Emma did re-appear at 4pm, but she refused me any contact with Charlie.

Sometimes Emma could get enough of a reaction out of me to ring the police, although later on she would just invent stuff when she felt like causing me trouble. On 5th December I had been splitting logs for the living room fire down at the farm buildings. I used some yellow buckets to carry the logs from the tractor link box to the house. Emma came over and accused me of lying when I explained what I was doing. When she brought Charlie over later for contact she decided to have a row about the yellow buckets. She refused to leave the room. When I raised my voice she made a grab for Charlie. I manhandled her out of the room and tried to take Charlie's shoes out of her hands. She insisted that she had to put them on him herself. So I bent her thumb back till she released the shoes. She went into the kitchen to ring the police. I took Charlie up to my bedroom and locked the door; Emma in hot pursuit. Amazingly the police only took ten minutes to arrive. Charlie was very nervous of the policemen. I spoke to two policemen in my bedroom with Charlie. They were not sure what to do, so they left. In retaliation I was denied contact with Charlie for a few days. Although Charlie, on two occasions, threw a tantrum when he saw me and could not get to me; he was always whisked away.

The firearms unit had come to impound Emma's illegally held revolver. It was a gun she had found in her father's safe after he died. I had refused to allow her to keep the bullets and had disposed of them, but she still had the gun. I asked the police if I could have Charlie for my contact time. They said they had taken Charlie to his grandmother's house. When I complained that he should be left with me the policeman replied that a judge would not have wanted him to interfere. I wanted to say that surely his job was to uphold court orders! But I didn't.

Once, I made a rare stand against Emma's bullying over contact. She had told me she was changing my contact time to the afternoon as she had an appointment with her solicitor in the morning. I told her it was not acceptable and contravened the contact order. In the morning I blocked her van in with my car. She phoned her solicitor and then the police. Two policemen arrived. I asked if I could tape the interview and they agreed. I produced the two court orders that detailed the contact times and the fact that Emma was not to be present at contact. I said I was quite happy for Emma to go to her solicitor's appointment but she would have to leave Charlie with me for the contact period. Emma refused saying I was dangerous. I suspect that because I was taping the exchanges the police read the documents carefully and then pointed out to Emma that if the judge had deemed me dangerous he would have ordered that we all remain on the property during contact. Emma refused to leave, so she missed her appointment. The police left when the contact period came to an end, and I moved my car. I did not see Charlie though. Emma tried to block my car in with her van, for days but I always left enough room to manoeuvre. I enjoyed her frustration! That evening Emma packed up and moved out to stay with her mother, claiming she had been advised by her solicitor, the CAFCASS officer and the health visitor to do that. I was doubtful.

One evening in March I was in my bedroom watching television with the dog. The door was ajar. Emma returned to the house with Charlie at about 8.15 pm and put Charlie to bed. As usual she carried Charlie to and from the bathroom so he could not see me. Emma came back to my room and tried to take the dog away. She was abusive and tried to wind me up. She ignored my requests to leave the room. Eventually I told her to "fuck off". She kept coming back to my room, so I shut the door in her face. She came in again to take the dog. I grabbed her hand and pushed her back out of the room. She stumbled and fell against the bathroom wall. She went downstairs and phoned the police.

A policeman and policewoman arrested me in my bedroom at about 10.30pm. I was not allowed to say anything and was driven to the police station. I waited with the policeman quite a while until the custody sergeant was ready. I was searched, and then booked in. I had to sign various forms then taken to a cell with a very bright light and left with two plastic cups of water. At about 3.15am I was taken for interview. The policewoman seemed very hesitant and inexperienced. I gave a long description of the incident on tape and then answered a few questions. At around 5am I was processed for finger prints, photographed and had a swab taken from my mouth for a DNA sample. I was then cautioned and told to wait outside the police station. I was then picked up by the policeman and woman and taken home. I was close to tears with the injustice of it all. I felt dirty, defiled and completely powerless.

I asked Emma for the child car seat for contact as the judge had ruled I could drive Charlie and leave the property for contact, to get some peace and quiet and time that we could enjoy together. Emma ignored repeated requests throughout the day. I had tried for days to get hold of the District Domestic Violence Liaison officer (DDVLO) at the police station. I went to another police station, but they insisted it was nothing to do with them. I patiently pointed out to them that if they or someone in authority could speak to Emma about her behaviour it might prevent a more serious incident when I finally lost my temper. They promised to contact the DDVLO and get her to contact me. Nothing happened. I had to wait well into my contact period before Emma supplied the car seat. I took Charlie to feed the ducks at the park. Later in the day I went back into town to buy another car seat. The next day I took Charlie and the dogs for a walk. Charlie seemed to thoroughly enjoy the woods and rough ground, frequently doing his comical little jigs in a circle saying zee, zee, zee, He always did that when he was happy. When we drove into the drive and before I could turn the engine off, Emma had yanked open Charlie's door and tried to pull him out. She was so angry that she seemed unable to deal with the car seat belt. I asked her to leave us and wait in the kitchen. Emma was screaming and sobbing with frustration yanking Charlie against the seat belt, trying to drag him from the car. Charlie was crying then screaming with pain so I forced Emma away, prizing her fingers off the sear belt. Eventually I got Charlie out and carried him to the back door, where Emma repeatedly tried to grab Charlie from me, all the time yelling abuse. I put Charlie down and Emma whisked him away. Emma's behaviour was disgraceful. Emma then refused to let me into the kitchen, blocking me physically with Charlie in her arms. She was very abusive. I backed off and rang the police. I explained the situation and was told a car would be sent. The police phoned me back and asked questions. I asked that the DDVLO contact me as soon as possible, as they were now refusing to send a car. I was assured that they would arrange it. They did not.

I finally had a meeting with the district domestic violence liaison officer. We talked for over an hour. She suggested that I approach social services to have a talk with Emma about her behaviour in front of Charlie. I also talked to the Citizen's Advice Bureau, and they arranged a meeting with social services for me. I saw the duty social worker for an hour. She promised to have a talk with Emma about her behaviour in front of Charlie. A week later I wrote a letter via her solicitor to Emma detailing all my concerns about her behaviour in front of Charlie and how damaging it was to Charlie. If Emma wanted something I was usually prepared to listen, unless she timed it to clash with something like my computer class. If I wanted to discuss something I was always told to do it through her solicitor.

In early May the police were called out over an incident with of all things, the washing machine. One of Emma's petty bullying tactics was to refuse to give me more than one set of sheets for my mattress on the floor. So I had to pick a day when I could wash and dry my sheets before I made the bed again. Just before I was due to have Charlie for contact and while Emma was having breakfast, I put the washing machine on for my sheets. Emma turned it off saying there was a problem with the water supply, and that she and Charlie were going to have a bath. She then claimed that Charlie's nappies had to go on first. I said that I needed to get my one pair of sheets washed and out to dry before I went out later. So I turned the machine back on. There was a tussle and I slowly pushed her away from the machine. She screamed that she would call the police. So I told her to go ahead. When she left I locked the connecting door from the kitchen to utility room and chained the back door. Sometime later the police arrived. In his discussion with me the policeman warned me that social services would not allow a bad situation for Charlie to continue indefinitely. When they had left and the washing was done Emma came over with a hammer and tried to knock the security chain off the door.

Emma often had to work late at night or very early in the morning. Partly because in the day she would waste a lot of time interfering with my contact time with Charlie and partly it appeared that she had staff problems. As a result she would come over to the house and make a lot of noise at all hours going in and out leaving doors open behind her. I told her it amounted to harassment. If she left the back door open there was a security problem. She used to put the washing machine on at 11pm or 5am. I told her I was going to lock the kitchen to utility room door at night. She could have access to the rest of the house during the day. At this time she was living with her mother in the next hamlet. She could unlock the back door to access the utility room and the washing machine. The next day I was awoken at 6.30 am by a policeman. I chatted to the policeman in the kitchen and explained what Emma had been doing. The policeman was sympathetic and left after fifteen minutes saying he would take no action. I wrote a long letter to the DDVLO. The dogs now spent most of the days locked in the van. Charlie was often locked in the van for long periods too.

A week after the visit by the policeman I drove up the drive to find Emma outside with the dogs. As the organic farm inspector arrived to do his inspection Emma was distracted. When I opened the estate car boot the dogs jumped in, and I decided I would take them for a long walk. Emma tried to stop me, but I finally appreciated the value of central locking. With her usual verbal abuse she stood in front of the car to prevent me from leaving. The drive had a very slight gradient. After staring at each other, listening to her call me an evil bastard for the nth time, I put the car gear into neutral and took my foot off the brake. The car rolled forward very slowly. Emma tried to stop it but was not strong enough, so she jumped onto the bonnet. I put the brake on and she slowly slid off the bonnet in an ungainly heap on the ground. I reversed up and drove round her. She later completely exaggerated the incident claiming I had actually run her over!

On the next contact date I arrived very early and looked down at the farm from the ridge road. There was smoke rising from the chimney in the house and the van was parked outside. I went into town to get a cup of tea. I turned up at the farm on time but now there was no one around. I waited an hour and then as I was driving out the entrance, Emma drove up in the van. I turned the car round and drove back up the drive behind her. Emma rushed over to the back door to unlock it and then ran back to Charlie's door of the van. I got out of my car and locked it as it had a lot of my legal papers inside. I went round to Charlie's side of the van. Emma had Charlie's door open. She backed up and turned to me. Belligerently she asked me what I was doing? I told her I had come to see Charlie as per the court order. She said I could not see Charlie as nothing had been sorted. I said there was nothing to sort as I had shown her the work contract letters demonstrating that I worked on Fridays, as she had requested and that in future I would see Charlie on Saturdays. As I was talking I got up to Charlie's door and squeezed between Emma and Charlie. Emma got very agitated and tried to pull me away. I was talking to Charlie and trying to unbuckle his seat belt. Emma started yelling and pounding her fists on my back. Charlie started to cry, so I turned and yelled at Emma to stop hitting me and to back off. She kept pushing, pulling and hitting me. So I pushed her backwards. Behind her was a pile of scalpings, and she lost her footing and stumbled into the corner wall of the house, with her right hand out to balance herself and then fell over onto the wheely bin. I undid the buckle on Charlie's seat belt and was trying to calm him, but I could not free him from all the seat belts. Emma came back really angry. She pummelled my back and then grabbed my arm and sleeve to pull me away. We tussled back and forth getting more heated, calling each other names. I said I would call the police and they could come and sort it. I managed to dial 999 as Emma tried to grab the phone out of my hand. When I got through Emma started to yell and scream for the police to come and save her son. I eventually got through to the local police but it was difficult to hear anything with Emma yelling all the time. I told her to wait for the police to come. But Emma kept on attacking me and trying to pull me away. At one point I turned and raised my fist and yelled at her to back off or I would hit her hard and it would really hurt. She ignored my threat. I closed Charlie's door. When Emma was pulling me hard, I turned and stepped towards her so she lost her balance. She stumbled over the pile of scalpings. She put out her hand again to break her fall. Then she fell over on to her front and her left hand scraped over the scalpings. She got up with a look of pure hatred and calmly said, "I am going to get an order to have you locked up and you are not going to come near me and when this is over you are never going to see Charlie again". She tried to get Charlie's door open but I blocked her. She then tried to open the sliding door to get to Charlie's door from the inside. I blocked her. She then said that the dogs needed to be let out. So I told her to open the rear doors. We calmed down, but we still set to over certain points. She said I was mental: I replied that she was sick and needed treatment, that she was like her mother, who really was sick and evil. She went on about me lying, so I challenged her to give some examples. She could not come up with a single incident. She repeatedly said that I was not Charlie's dad and bizarrely claimed I had told a walker that he was not mine. I said that technically I was not his father, but then neither was she technically Charlie's mother. Charlie had quietened down and was sucking his thumb, looking at me. Eventually Emma and I faced off three feet apart leaning against the van.

The police arrived about 20 minutes after I phoned them. Immediately Emma started to cry and sob that they must save her son from me. A young policeman took Emma inside the house. The sergeant spoke to me. I took Charlie out of the van and cuddled him. I gave a brief account of events and the sergeant suggested we went into the house. I stayed in the utility room with Charlie. I had to fetch the contact orders and two pay slips. On the radio they got confirmation of the previous contact order. I was left with Charlie for a while and we hugged and laughed. He had settled down. It tore me apart that he was subjected to all this hostility all the time. The police returned and said they were duty bound to arrest me as Emma had a slight graze on her left hand. I was taken to the police station.

After being processed I was put in a cell at about midday. At 3.10pm the duty solicitor arrived and we had a chat. I was then interviewed on tape with the solicitor present. I got tearful at the end out of sheer frustration at the law. I had my fingerprints taken, was charged with common assault and told to attend the Magistrate's court. I drove home emotionally exhausted. I duly appeared at the Magistrate's court. After giving my name, address and date of birth in the dock, I asked for a plea of not guilty. Bail was to remain. One of the policemen was to be a witness for Emma. So we had to wait hours for dates to be agreed with him for a trial date. Before I left I asked the Magistrate to clarify contact. His answer was that there would be none till the Family court addressed the matter.

These incidents largely made up my contact with the police throughout the time that I was having a struggle with my wife at home, before I moved out. Once I had moved out these naturally stopped. My impression was that the police try take a softly softly approach but are prepared to respond robustly and always to show bias on the side of the woman in these situations. This is understandable to a certain extent because although men are victims of domestic violence, by and large women will always be more vulnerable.

I found individual officers who dealt with me to be courteous and in some cases sympathetic but as an arm of the law in cases such as mine they are, from my standpoint, ineffectual. My ex-wife would, I am sure, tell a different story!

Chapter Five

DIARY

I have often heard it said that keeping a diary during any traumatic event can be helpful. It can help to get things into perspective and to vent frustrations if you can actually get things down on paper or into a computer file. It can also help, if like me you need to remember specifics for court cases.

The events that I have recorded in these chapters are made up of my diary of events for some of the time and by and large they tell their own story. They are all true and when I read them back now it is hard for me to believe that I did not see sooner just what downright hate fuelled determination I was up against.

I have included them here so that those of you reading my account of what happened during just part of my long struggle to have a relationship with my son will understand better the way things went for me.

June 12th, Wednesday.

Big row with Emma. I tell her I am exhausted mentally and physically and desperately need to take a week off to recharge my batteries.

I explain that she would have to cover for me the next week and arrange for Greg the stockman to look after the farm at the weekend. Emma said she had already arranged to have a barbeque at her cousin's to celebrate Charlie's first birthday. I felt incredibly irritated not to have been consulted. I explain that it would have to be next week or not at all for my break because of all the business problems. Our most experienced dairy worker was going on holiday, clashing with the local festival week. Also the weather forecast suggested a window for haymaking was coming up soon. I said my health was more important than driving four hours to go to a party. She needed to understand the gravity of the situation: I would leave on Saturday. Apparently she didn't give a fig.

June 14th, Friday.

Charlie's birthday. I manage to see him awake between delivery rounds mid-morning. How he has grown in a year! Emma still very frosty and difficult. She decides to go to Sussex with the dogs in the van for the weekend.

June 15th, Saturday.

I heard Charlie and Emma leave very early. I went back to sleep. Up at 8 am to discover the car has gone. Thinking of hiring a car for the week, I check the cash box. Shocked to discover there is less than £100 pounds and no credit card. There is usually about a thousand in the box. I realised I have been set up. I am hurt and perplexed at the implications.

June 24th, Monday.

With our senior dairy worker on holiday, Emma had no choice but to help out part-time in the dairy. She finally understood and agreed to getting a part-time worker to help out, as soon as possible.

June 27th, Thursday.

Talked to Greg about the local festival. He confirmed that he would milk the goats over the weekend so that I could concentrate on getting the hay bales into the barns by Sunday, when rain was forecast. The contractors will finish baling tomorrow. I asked him to keep an eye out for field invasions and vandalism. It looks like yet again there will be no time to go to the festival with our free tickets.

June 28th, Friday.

Got back late from deliveries at about 8pm because of the festival traffic. Emma told me Greg has walked out. Bizarrely she said that he refused to talk to me, and if I went round to see him, he would "knock me out cold"! He does not answer his phone. I am pretty angry at what I assumed to be one of Greg's stunts. I was worried about getting all the hay in before the rain came. I did not want to think of the consequences if I had to do all the farm work as well as run the dairy and do all the deliveries, especially with some staff still on holiday for the coming week.

June 30th, Sunday.

A very long day. Managed to get all the hay in from the in-bye fields and built giant stacks in the outlying fields. Ended up milking late evening. Wind moved round to the south so could hear the festival music loud and clear.

July 1st, Monday.

A new worker starts part-time. One girl spends all her time in the house looking after Charlie. Emma starts to organise the staff as I am spending much time with the farm work. When I turn up to help, Emma goes back to the house!

July 3rd, Wednesday.

The dairy products were not ready yesterday so I have to deliver after morning milking. Everything is so rushed. On the return I pull over to a lay-by and write a letter explaining what I think is needed to reorganise our lives and hopefully save our marriage. The main thrust is the need to reduce my stress levels as the doctors and therapists are demanding. I consider that we should sell all the rare breed cattle, pigs and sheep and reduce the amount of land we rent. I would milk the goats five days a week, and have nothing to do with the processing side of the business. This would leave me some time to finish off building the house and sort the garden out. I would also consider being a househusband if Emma wanted to run the whole business. I ask for an answer within three days. I explain the letter to Emma in the evening.

July 5th, Friday.

Start milking at 4.30 a.m. to get away on deliveries as early as possible. Emma refuses to deal with the fresh milk, so I dump it in the house field. Such a waste. I rush off to do the deliveries. Emma and I have appointment with homoeopath and hypnotherapist at 2.15 pm for joint discussion on our problems and marriage. My hypnotherapist takes charge of the meeting and asks me to say what I wanted for the future and what it is that I still find attractive and love in Emma. I say that I want a future with Emma and Charlie. I want to be involved in bringing up Charlie, and to that end I need to reduce my working hours. If necessary I would consider getting a normal job to help achieve this and give up the business. I say I still found Emma attractive and desirable especially when she was in her feminine and caring role. I loved that we still had so many common attitudes and standards. The hypnotherapist asked Emma to explain what she wanted and liked about me. Emma explained at length what she wanted for her and Charlie. After a few minutes the hypnotherapist interrupted her and explained that she had spent all of her time talking about Charlie but not a word about me. Emma said it was taken for granted that she wanted me included. So the hypnotherapist asked her to talk specifically about me. After a long silence the hypnotherapist gently coaxed Emma with questions. Eventually, after getting no responses the hypnotherapist asked Emma just to say what she still saw in me. Emma suddenly burst into tears and rushed out of the room. I made to follow but the homoeopath said he would go after her. The hypnotherapist asked what I made of that. I replied that I had never seen Emma burst into tears like that before. She always came to tears slowly. It was a big issue for Emma to remain in control of her emotions at all times. The hypnotherapist stated bluntly that in her opinion she thought that the action was faked. Emma had used the outburst to get out of the situation because she plainly could not answer the questions. She said there was a lot more underlying this. As we had an appointment for tomorrow, she ended the session there. I rushed back to the farm, loaded up the deliveries and sped off. I got to the last shop just as they were locking up. I got home at 8.30pm. I was so tired that I decided just to feed and check the animals. I milked all the newly kidded goatlings by hand in their pen. I shut the gates so the goats could not go back out to the fields.

July 6th, Saturday.

I start milking at 4am. I check all the livestock. Then I rush out to the fields to bring all the remaining hay in to the barns, before they get seriously damaged by rain. After supper I asked Emma to answer the questions the hypnotherapist had asked her. For one and a half hours she evades answering the questions. Eventually she exclaims that there was no future between us: there is too much water under the bridge. She explained that she had no feelings for me anymore. After much thought I said that I could not conceive of living with somebody that had no positive feelings for me. I agree to end the marriage. I ask that we split amicably.

July 7th, Sunday.

For some reason Emma is very hostile all day. In the evening she denies our conversation took place yesterday, and refuses to acknowledge that we had a meeting with the therapists on Friday. I get quite angry. I say I am fed up with all the lies and untruths since Charlie was born. I do not understand it. I had complete faith and trust in her till Charlie was about to appear. In fact her honesty and rectitude were the traits I loved most about her.

July 9th, Tuesday.

Emma drives off with Charlie early, and returns alone. When questioned, Emma tells me she has taken Charlie to nursery school. I was really angry for not being included at all. Charlie is far too young to go to nursery for half a day. It is an obvious ploy to keep Charlie away from me as much as possible.

July 10th, Wednesday.

During Monday and Tuesday Emma is very hostile, frosty and critical. We had a spot organic inspection from UKROFS, so I ended up milking late. When I was washing up the supper things I tried to talk about this hostility. It degenerated into a row about the continued unpleasantness. She tells me to leave, to get out. I remind her that there are 170 goats to milk, and I am the only person capable of milking them, plus all the other livestock. She coolly tells me that I can leave anytime as she has arranged with Greg to cover things when I am gone. She goaded me to try and make me go, so I told her to get Greg to milk tomorrow afternoon onwards and to tell him to check the message board in the parlour.

July11th, Thursday.

I milk the goats and check all the stock. There had been torrential rain overnight and Betty, a large white sow is about to farrow. She had built her nest in a hollow and it has filled up with water. Betty is a moody pig, sometimes she would stand to have her ears scratched and nudge you playfully: other times she would attack. She was in a foul mood so I decided not to leave her to Greg to sort out. On another occasion Greg and I had to move her and we tried to use an extremely heavy 5 bar metal gate to guide her. She flipped the gate straight over our heads. Luckily she attacked the gate in the mud and we both escaped over the electric fence. I built her a new dry house on a rising bit of ground. When I was ready to leave Emma refused to give me the car keys. I had taken the precaution of keeping the van keys. So I said I would take that instead and she would have to hire a van for the deliveries. I pointed out that she could not drive both. She said she had had my name removed from the insurance for the car. She rang the police for help. They declined to get involved unless someone was injured. She rang our solicitor, who eventually advised her to reinstate the insurance and swap the keys over. Emma was nearly apoplectic at having been outsmarted, and drove off in the van with Charlie. She threatened to change the house locks when I told her I had taken £220 from the cash box. She said I would not see Charlie again. I had a quick word with the staff. They were concerned for Charlie, and very sorry that Emma was being so difficult to everyone. Mother was not at home so I went and stayed at my uncle's house. I had a bad night, up 7 times.

July 15th, Monday.

Receive divorce papers from Emma. Uncle J suggests that I get some advice from his solicitor.

July 18th, Thursday.

See a lady solicitor, who explains the procedures in divorce.

July 20th, Saturday.

Hypnotherapist at 9.30am. Good hand warming session. Called in at the farm to see Charlie. Nobody in, so took the dogs for a long walk. On returning, Emma is very frosty, Charlie is teething. Cousin staying to help out. I help deliver a steer to a butcher locally. Try to discuss short and medium term future. Emma insists on taping conversation. She is so aggressive and argumentative. On leaving I ask for a cheque so that I can pay the solicitor to reply to the divorce petition. Emma refuses and when I find the spare chequebook she becomes physically aggressive, in front of Charlie and the cousin. Emma threatens to call the police; so I say please do. Emma says she will call her solicitor on Monday and also stop the cheque. I leave, bewildered.

July 22nd, Monday.

Give cheque for £400 to new solicitor to reply to divorce action. I drive down to my sister's home to house sit whilst she goes on holiday for a fortnight.

July 28th, Sunday.

I phone Emma to say I would call in tomorrow to see Charlie. She says I cannot see Charlie during the week, as it was not convenient. They would also be away next weekend. I told her I was returning to the farm on the 6th, next week.

July 29th, Monday.

Ring the cousin to try to get some explanation for Emma's aggression and attitude. Although technically she was Emma's cousin's widow, she had always been the only relative who was friendly to me. In the previous six months she had come down to stay to help Emma with Charlie on several occasions. She had offered and acted as a marriage mediator to help us solve our problems, claiming to be impartial as she was not actually a relative. She knew much of our problems. Although we spoke for 20 minutes, she made it plain that she had now sided with Emma and was unable to help. I felt very let down by her attitude.

August 6th, Tuesday.

Return to the farm at midday to a barrage of abuse from Emma. Said I should have been back at 6am to milk. Emma lays down the law saying I cannot enter our bedroom or Charlie's room. Charlie is subtly kept away from me: even when the wholesaler's lorry came for the evening pick-up. Emma took Charlie still eating cheese over to the dairy. I am quite shocked at the constant verbal abuse, even in front of Charlie.

August 7th, Wednesday.

I spend the day trying to sort out the mess at the farm. Find our bull about 2km down the valley. Realise there is a cow missing and eventually find her in the woods having given birth to a calf in the last few days. Rounded up the sheep that had gone walkabout on neighbour's fields. Must move all the pigs onto fresh ground as soon as possible. Emma is very abusive when I refuse to help in the dairy, as we had agreed. I had to push Emma out of the way in front of the staff when she tried to physically stop me saying hello to Charlie. I pick him up and take him over to the house. Emma storms out, and the staff cheer! They say it is time I put my foot down! I explain that I found it really difficult to confront Emma in front of Charlie. Emma retaliates by telling me that I cannot have the credit card to buy a mobile phone, and she will deduct house-keeping from my wages. I tell her she has no control over the company money.

August 8th, Thursday.

Emma and Charlie home very late from deliveries. I ring the staff to see if the round was done differently. They tell me there is a mobile number in the dairy. It goes straight to voice mail. So I ring our mechanic to see if he had been called out to a breakdown. He hadn't. So I rang the last shopkeeper on the round at his home. He tells me that Emma had left the shop at 7.45pm. I am in the bath when they return. I am completely dumfounded by Emma's response when I explain that what I had done I did because I was concerned for them. The torrent of verbal abuse screamed at me with Charlie half asleep in her arms was disgraceful. I begin to wonder if this aggression is really, as I assumed, temporary.

August 10th, Saturday.

Milking takes so long that I miss my hypnotherapy session. I decide to give the kitchen a proper clean. On moving the bread bin I find a letter addressed to me from the business bank dated a month earlier, informing me that, on instructions from Emma, they had removed my signature from the account. Cheques signed by me would no longer be honoured! I went ballistic. When Emma reappeared she gloated that she now has financial control of the business. I would be paid for any work I did on the farm, and she would not pay for any other farm staff. I replied that I did not think what had happened was legal, and I would sort it out on Monday. I realise that her behaviour and attitude to the divorce had turned from unpleasant to nasty. I assume part of the reason for her aggression and abuse stems from her feeling guilt for her behaviour. By the end of the day I am aware of a shift from the personal verbal abuse to a more constant criticism of how I run the farm.

August 12th, Monday.

The bank is adamant their action is legal and say they will defend it in court if necessary. I discover that our personal joint account is empty. So I arrange to open a personal bank account and order a mobile phone. My sister is very supportive and will lend me money till I can sort the problem out. Emma and I have a big row in the evening. She just won't let go. I feel quite bruised and down. I decide that it may be best if I find somewhere to rent nearby till the farm is sold. I am not sure if we can afford it.

August 13th, Tuesday.

Greg appears at afternoon milking asking if he can come back to work. I tell him I had been told that he could no longer work with me. He said he didn't know where I had got that idea from. He needed to work to pay the rent. I tell him that Emma runs the business now and he will have to square it with her. He could milk part-time and help do the big jobs like emptying the barns of all the deep litter from last winter. Emma agrees for him to cover my two days off a week and some jobs. Can I believe him? Can I trust him? No.

August 22nd, Thursday.

Greg off ill Monday to Wednesday. Says the level of stress has brought on his MS. He insists on milking today and tomorrow on my days off. Half way through milking he rushes off to the doctor in great pain. I finish milking and feed the stock. Greg reappears having had an injection to kill the pain. He insists I go off to my appointment with my solicitor. I give him my mobile number and tell him I can come back anytime.

Solicitor says that Emma is not actively engaged in her divorce petition. If I want to see Charlie unhindered then I have to get a contact order. Apparently to do that I need to petition for divorce myself. I instruct her to petition for divorce on grounds of unreasonable behaviour and apply for a contact order. Uncle gives me a deposit for the solicitors to get started.

August 23rd, Friday.

Greg rings me to say he needs the weekend to recuperate. I tell him I do not expect him back till Monday. When I return to the farm Emma tells me that Greg had said he could no longer work for us. Emma said she was taking Charlie to visit her cousin in Sussex for the weekend. I had to do all the preparatory work for the dairy on Sunday. I told her I did not work in the dairy anymore.

August 24th, Saturday.

At the end of milking Greg appeared to tell me that he could no longer work for us, but if I asked him nicely he may cover my two days off a week. I told him I would make other arrangements. I've decided to milk the goats once a day from now on. Emma left at 9.30am. As Charlie is never in his room, I decide to move my stuff and have it as my bedroom. Charlie continues to sleep in Emma's bed. I disapprove!

August 25th, Sunday.

Emma returns home at 10pm. She is really angry that I have moved into Charlie's room. She puts Charlie to bed and puts the barricade up in her bedroom doorway so Charlie cannot get out. (None of the rooms upstairs have doors fitted yet). Amidst a torrent of verbal abuse Emma demands that she has the chest of drawers. I tell her to take whatever she wants. She is yelling and screaming at me. She goes into the spare bedroom and starts throwing all the large empty boxes across into my room. I get out of bed to stop the boxes, when Charlie starts screaming from the barricade. I go and pick him up to cuddle and quieten him. Emma realises that I have Charlie and comes bounding out of the spare bedroom yelling and screaming at me to give Charlie to her. I ask her to back off and calm down for Charlie's sake. She tries to pull Charlie out of my arms; I put my arm out to hold her at bay and then she starts hitting and slapping me. It is obvious that she is not going to stop and the situation is making Charlie more upset, so I hand Charlie over to her. She rushes downstairs with Charlie and phones the police. I go back to bed. Two police cars arrive. I stay in bed. There was a lot of laughter coming from downstairs. I get up and meet a policeman on the stairs and ask how long they expect to remain in the house. I am told to stay upstairs and a constable comes up to listen to my side of the story and to see the scene. Emma tells them I have two shotguns, so they impound those, along with her airgun. I do not say anything about her illegally held .38 revolver. They want to arrest me for domestic violence but Emma says I have to milk the goats in the morning. She never worked on the farm. I was very shocked and then angry that the police assumed I was guilty.

August 28th, Wednesday.

Greg comes in to beg for work. Offer him odd jobs and the two days off for me.

August 29th, Thursday.

Staff off ill, very surprised to see Greg working in the dairy. Hygiene is not his strong point! After deliveries Emma dumps Charlie on me. Great! Give him supper and bath and put him to bed. Emma keeps coming over to check up and goes over the top that I had put Charlie's night time nappy and liner on inside out and apparently his pyjamas back to front. I try to reason with her, asking that she show me how to do some things instead of just criticising all the time. I point out that she had lots of help and instruction at the maternity unit after Charlie was born. Just got a constant tirade that I was not fit to look after children. Even after Charlie was in bed, Emma kept up constant unpleasantness about cleaning the house. She tries very hard to get a rise out of me; she certainly winds me up.

August 31st, Saturday.

Greg comes up for his pay and asks me what work is available for next week. Emma says she will not pay for any work next week.

September 7th, Saturday.

Greg appears in the middle of milking to ask that his work situation is sorted as, if not, he will have to find a job elsewhere soon. I tell him I will sort it. Emma refuses to talk about it. I write a letter to Emma saying that Greg's position, as a worker has to be addressed. I also said I am not prepared to work for nothing. If I do not get access to the company money, then I have to be paid as she had said. I was not going to exist on borrowed money from my family. If I did not have an answer in writing by tomorrow evening then I will no longer work in the business.

September 9th, Monday.

At 7am I ask Emma for an answer to my ultimatum. She says no. At 7.30am Greg rings and Emma asks him to work full time looking after the farm. At last, proof that they are working in league together. At 8.45am I ask Emma to clear one of the desks so that I can get on and sort the accounts as she has made an application for legal aid in her divorce case. She refuses so I start to clear one of them. She tries to block me physically. So I push her out of the way. She rings the police, claiming that I have assaulted her. Police car arrives at 9.30am. The sergeant was very helpful and gave me lots of advice. He said he had been there, done that, got the tee shirt. He said I could not win in any situation like this. I should go and do the work somewhere else, like the library. All of these incidents will be used by her legal team to fight my access to Charlie. His partner has talked to Emma. He came over to say that Emma felt nervous with me present. They ask me to leave the farm for the day. I go to visit my sister. I feel despair that there seems little I can do to stop Emma's bullying. The solicitor has no answers.

September 11th, Wednesday.

Up early to prepare for court appearance. Smell a rat as Emma stays in bed late. Meet my lady barrister. She seems to have a grasp of the situation. Go before a lady District judge who reminds me of Betty Boothroyd. Whilst waiting for Emma to turn up, judge skims through the documents. Her demeanour changes visibly when she notes that the police have been involved. My counsel seems unable to get a word in. I ask if I can say a word. With a withering look the judge tells me to speak only when spoken to by her and today to keep my mouth shut. She adjourns the case for a fortnight.

September 12th, Thursday.

Drive up to see solicitor to finalise the divorce petition and Ancillary Relief (finances). Decide to spend the next few days seeing dad. Notice how frail he is becoming.

September 15th, Sunday.

When driving back to the farm, at 2.30pm Greg rings me to say he will not work on the farm anymore. I tell him it is not my problem anymore. Emma not at home so I leave a note about Greg's latest walk-out. Emma returns at 10.30pm with Charlie.

September 16th, Monday.

Emma is very unpleasant and abusive. I refuse to milk the goats but agree to feed and check all the stock. She discloses that she, the company, has a summons in the small claims court for non-payment of a bill. This really angers and saddens me as I have never been a late payer, especially to other small businesses. Reputation is important to me. I offer to look after Charlie the next day. Emma goes off on a rant at how dangerous I am to Charlie. She is going to deny me access and contact. Charlie is now barricaded in his room or taken over to the dairy to keep him away from me.

A man comes to milk the goats at 7.30pm, and leaves at midnight.

September 18th, Wednesday.

Emma refuses to provide any information to get the accounts up to date or to do the VAT return, which will provide the information requested for the legal aid. Decide to start work on establishing a garden and finishing off the inside of the house. Emma is very aggressive and anti this. Surprised to see Greg working on the farm again, so I ask him why. He says he is working for Emma now. I say it is nothing to do with me. He tries to accuse me of cruelty to animals for not milking the goats. I pointed out that it was his habit of walking out and being so unreliable that was the problem. He becomes very abusive so I walk away. I ask Emma, in front of the staff, if I can take Charlie for a walk. I am told I am too dangerous to be left alone with Charlie! In the evening I try to discuss the use of a mediator. Eventually after challenging excuse after excuse, Emma says she is not interested in mediation.

September 21st, Saturday.

I get up before Emma and have breakfast. Emma has barricaded the top of the stairs so Charlie can play over all the upstairs. Charlie starts crying so I go up to cuddle him. Emma is on the loo. Charlie quietened and snuggled into me. Emma hurries off the loo and demands I hand over Charlie, as I am dangerous and know nothing about toddlers. I continue to comfort Charlie, so Emma becomes abusive and shouting. Charlie upset again so I put him down and back off. As she takes Charlie downstairs Emma continues to rant "that man is a liar, sick, dangerous and useless". She carries on for a long time downstairs, repeatedly returning to the bottom of the stairs to yell at me. In desperation I show her that I am taping her diatribe on a Dictaphone. Miraculously she stops! Later Charlie is taken off the farm and left somewhere for several hours. Emma refuses to tell me where.

Later in the day I do my round of the farm checking up on things. The sheep are in a neighbour's field. Some of the cattle have gone walkabout too. The pig's electric fencing is down and piglets are ranging all over the house field, digging it up. I find the bulk tank room and milking parlour doors locked. When I ask Emma why, she says it is because I have been sabotaging the equipment! She wants to know why I go around inspecting things. I say I did not spend twenty years building a business to have it ruined by idiots, and if things deteriorated too much I would act. I leave notes to Emma about the problems and things to do on the farm, if she chooses to ignore my advice that is her decision.

September 23rd, Monday.

Charlie is kept in the dairy all day until I go to my computer class at 7pm. Ask Emma for the password to the computer so that I can practise. She refuses. I despair at the petty spite and animosity from Emma. I just wish I knew where it came from and why. Emma tells me I have to have her permission to take our dogs for a walk, because of the way I treat animals. Yeah, right. She never complained in the last 18 years!

September 25th, Wednesday.

Court hearing adjourned today. Emma argues that I am too dangerous to leave alone with Charlie. The judge disagrees and orders contact for one hour a day, without Emma present. Emma declares in court that she thinks mediation is a good idea and agrees to attend.

September 26-29th,

Emma ignores the court order for contact, and removes Charlie for the set times. Emma is so obnoxious that if it were not for the contact order I would go and stay at my sister's house for a few days. Tries to stop me taking the dogs for a walk and calls the police. Every time I put the washing machine on, she turns it off. I am constantly ordered to clean the house, do the shopping etc. In order to disrupt my appointment with the hypnotherapist, she dumps Charlie on me at the last minute, so I am late. Now insists that I have my meals separately and in another room if she is feeding Charlie.

Where is all this going? What effect is it having on Charlie? Discuss a lot of this with the hypnotherapist. Worrying!

September 30th, Monday.

Emma takes Charlie over to the dairy as soon as he gets up, in his pyjamas and with no breakfast! No happy birthday to me from Emma. Charlie brought over for contact and promptly falls asleep. Emma changes the mediation appointment to October 25th. At the end of contact Emma wakes Charlie up and takes him back to dairy.

October 1st, Tuesday.

Whilst Emma is in the bath Charlie comes into my room. Emma livid and comes in and yanks Charlie off the floor and drags him out, crying. Emma has changed tactics and has been leaving everything for me to clear up after her. Kitchen is disgusting, but I am not going to be her slave. Put the dishwasher on, Emma comes in and says she is going to report me to her solicitor for only having it half full. If I laugh I think she will have a full-blown tantrum. Charlie spends morning at nursery. Brought over at 4pm for contact, but very tired and sleepy. Emma appears at 4.45pm and disrupts contact saying she needs to find a map. Constant unpleasantness that Charlie picks up on. I go to put Charlie to sleep in his cot. Emma very aggressive and pulls Charlie away, yells at me to get out of her room. Taped a long tirade in the evening when she called me a maniac all the time. Pot, kettle and black! Up 4 or 5 times a night now, difficult to get back to sleep each time. Exhausting!

October 3rd, Thursday.

Charlie grisly with a cold but goes off to nursery for the morning. I clean the sitting room and am washing the kitchen floor when Emma storms in and turns the dishwasher off. I turn it on, she turns it off. She opens it and loads it with dirty saucepans, and puts the rest in the utility sink. I put the machine back on, push her out of the room and hold the door shut. She rings the police. They are busy and will come later. I get an appointment to see the G.P. I explain my concerns that it is inappropriate to keep Charlie in the dairy now that it is cold and much of the time it is unheated. He has got a cold. Also the routine is not good for him. GP says there is nothing he can do. Charlie does not have a regular routine, it is dependent on what work Emma is doing. No regular meal times or regular bedtime. I find it baffling that she would rather Charlie suffer than let me look after him, unless she wants to disrupt something I am doing. I strongly disapprove that Emma takes Charlie off on deliveries all day, obviously leaving him in the van when actually delivering and waiting to be paid.

October 4th, Friday.

Emma announces that Charlie will be going to nursery more from next week. I disapprove and point out that it contravenes the contact order. She doesn't care. Says I can see Charlie between 4 and 5pm instead. What a surprise, Charlie is usually exhausted by that time. Emma drives off with Charlie and the dogs at 5.30pm. Doesn't tell me she is going away for the week-end. Leaves the dairy locked up, to prevent me getting fresh milk etc. Find a way in through the back.

October 5th, Saturday.

Discover all the papers pertaining to the impounding of my guns have gone missing, so go to the police station to deal with it. I am getting very fed up with Emma's antics. Hang the door on my bedroom and fit the lock. I am nervous about what level Emma will get to with her aggression. Hypnotherapist and sister tell me never to turn my back on Emma. She is very possibly psychotic and could be dangerous.

October 7th, Monday.

Charlie to nursery, Emma says she has staff problems, there's a surprise! Contact refused. Later Charlie dumped on me, great. I ask for his Wellingtons. Told he cannot walk well in them so refused. I said all the more reason for him to practise! I have taken to going outside if weather good to have contact in peace. Latest ploy to stop this is to lock the socks, shoes and coat in the van. Emma gets some bread out of the freezer and pins a note to say it is just for her and Charlie. I have to laugh seeing as I bought it! I put all Emma's dirty pots and pans out on the patio. Play pen no longer used in dairy. Now the weather is colder Charlie spends all the time in his pram in a child's sleeping bag!

October 15th, Tuesday.

See the health care visitor about my concerns for Charlie. She outright does not believe me and says Emma is an excellent mum. She refuses to talk to the staff. I suppose that as Emma has seen her regularly for over a year, she had already spun a lot of lies about me. I am now aware that a lot of locals distance themselves so I assume I have been well briefed against. It is beginning to seem like it is a campaign for Emma. The kitchen is the latest battleground. Whenever I start to prepare supper Emma arrives and demands the kitchen to make Charlie's supper. I now wait to have breakfast after they have gone to the dairy. For the first time in ages she cleans up after supper including the dirty pots and pans outside. Guess she realises that I will not be pushed around if it does not affect Charlie directly.

October 18th, Friday.

Emma is on the warpath. She goes to the doctor. Tells me to look after Charlie, then drives off on deliveries with him. No contact again (3rd time this week). Find a note on my bedroom door, after walking the dogs. Tells me to work on the farm from Monday and to prepare all the dairy stuff on Sunday ready for Monday. Tell her I will consult my solicitor on Monday, but unlikely to do any work for her without a written agreement. Charlie is kept out of my way.

October 19th, Saturday.

Frosty is an understatement. Charlie comes to my room and bangs on the door twice. Emma very angry and hauls Charlie downstairs screaming. Shocked that she literally drags Charlie like a rag doll, repeating a mantra that "that man is dangerous, spiteful, nasty and sick." I can't have contact because she can't risk having Charlie being locked in my room.

October 20th, Sunday.

Emma denies contact hour. Later I manage to play with Charlie for a bit. I am concerned that Charlie is crying a lot at nights. He is no longer teething. Emma says she is taking Charlie to have tea with some friends, odd, as they leave at 5.30pm.

October 21st, Monday.

When I get up in the night I realise something is wrong when all the lights are still on at 2am. There is no message from Emma. No sign of Greg in the morning, so realise this is planned. See the staff and tell them that unless Emma returns today, they can take it they are on a week's notice and I shall be closing down the business. I take them home. I speak to my solicitor, expressing my concern that Emma has done a runner with Charlie. On her advice I contact the Police Child protection Unit and report them missing. They ring back in 20 minutes to say they have located them and had been assured by Emma's solicitor that they will return to the farm today, and I will have my contact hour. They turn up at 4pm, Emma refuses to allow contact.

October 22nd, Tuesday.

See to the stock. Gun licensing policeman visits to check out the gun cabinet. Half way through contact Emma appears and is verbally abusive. She refuses to leave. Charlie is playing with his train trolley. He falls off and cries out. Emma demands that I give him to her. I tell her to leave. On the point of losing my temper so I dash into the kitchen with Charlie and close the door and block it. Emma dashes out the front door and runs around to the back door to come into the kitchen. I rush upstairs with Charlie and lock us in my bedroom. Emma bangs on the door for ages then goes downstairs to call the police.

October 23rd, Wednesday.

Feed the animals then pack a bag to stay with uncle. See my solicitor.

October 24th, Thursday.

Return to farm. Emma very unpleasant, asks about solicitor: "spend the night with her did you? Does she charge by the hour?" I march into the dairy and pick Charlie up for contact and walk out. Emma doesn't say a word in front of the staff.

October 25th, Friday.

Emma and I meet for the mediation appointment. Lady sees us together first, then Emma, then me on our own. At the end she declares that mediation is pointless and better to return to the court. Refused contact in the afternoon. (Next day too).

October 28th, Monday.

I am washing the kitchen floor when Emma brings Charlie over for contact. She declares that I cannot look after Charlie and wash the floor, so takes him back to the dairy. Comes over in the afternoon and asks if I want Charlie. I say yes, but because I am hoovering the sitting room, she takes Charlie back again.

October 29th, Tuesday.

Drive up to Norwich with sister and mum to a cousin's funeral. Emma refuses to make up the lost contact. Dad is barely talking to us, and his partner refuses to say hello. Don't know what that is about!

October 31st, Thursday.

Emma announces that Charlie is spending all day at nursery, so cannot have contact. Charlie goes straight to bed on return. Emma spends the evening trying to wind me up.

November 1st and 2nd, week-end.

Emma and Charlie away, so no contact. Back at 11.30pm. Charlie cries till 2am. Cries a lot at night. He is obviously not a happy bunny.

November 4th, Tuesday.

Owner of Charlie's nursery rings to tell me that Social Services have advised her not to release Charlie to me at the nursery unless I am on the list approved by Emma. I am incensed and so is my solicitor, when I ring her. Emma refuses to put me on the list. The staff are evidently embarrassed by the row we have in the dairy. Feel very low and frustrated. Emma refuses contact again.

November 6th, Wednesday.

Charlie at nursery all day, contact denied.

November 10th, Sunday.

Contact denied, no reason given.

November 11th, Monday.

Third contact hearing to address the breaches. The two barristers fail to make a deal. Sticking points appear to be over Christmas contact, all day nursery on Mondays and Wednesdays, and Emma is demanding judge stop me from driving a vehicle with Charlie in it. The judge refuses an interim hearing to sort any of this, leaving it to the final hearing. Judge asks if violence will be a consideration for the final hearing. Amazed to hear Emma's barrister announce that they were going to fight on the grounds that I am cruel to animals therefore I was a danger to Charlie. It was a laughable suggestion but they are serious. The judge gives them 21 days to submit allegations and witness statements. My legal team say they had never heard of a case like it. I ask my barrister to appeal over an interim hearing, as the judge has given me two hours contact times and I wanted to go off the farm to avoid the constant disruptions by Emma. He strongly advised against appealing, solicitor agrees with him. Charlie is having tantrums nearly every day now. Worrying.

November 16th, Saturday.

Emma changes tactic and plays music really loud in the kitchen, so Charlie keeps going to investigate. Contact almost impossible. I do not stop Charlie from being with Emma as I believe it is not good to cause friction in front of him. Unfortunately Emma is exploiting this all the time. It is so frustrating that she appears to have no conscience, nor care about her actions and how they affect Charlie. I wonder whether I should talk to Social Services.

December 5th, Thursday.

In the morning I go down to the barn and split logs for the fire. I use some yellow buckets to carry the logs to the tractor link box. Emma appears and demands to know what I am doing. I show her, she does not believe me. I take a load up to the house. When she brings Charlie over for contact she argues about the yellow buckets. I ask her repeatedly to leave. She refuses and seems determined to have a row about the buckets. She succeeds in winding me up so that I raise my voice. She declares that I cannot have contact and goes to take Charlie away. I push her out of the sitting room. She insists that she has to put Charlie's shoes on his feet. So I bend her fingers back till she releases the shoes. She goes back into the kitchen to ring the police. I dash upstairs with Charlie and lock the bedroom door. Emma is hot on my heels and demands I open the door. I ignore her banging on the door. Obviously Charlie is upset. Ten minutes later a policeman asked to come in the bedroom. I was interviewed by two policemen. Charlie was nervous of them. After explaining what has happened they leave.

December 6th and 7th.

Drive down to stay with friends in Cornwall for the week-end. Before returning mid-morning on Monday I get two phone calls from a scaffold company telling me that Emma will not accept the delivery. I instruct them to leave it anyway. All the decorating and dry lining work I am doing to finish off the inside of the house, Emma tries to ruin. I just do not understand her animosity or why she wants to continue to live in a tip. On my return I discover that Emma has fitted burglar chains to the back and front doors. I realise there is a good chance I may get locked out. Contact denied.

Discover that Emma has reunited with her mother after an earlier acrimonious split and she takes Charlie to her to keep him away from me in the house. The dairy is too cold at times. Snow today!

December 11th, Wednesday.

Go to get the post from the front gate. Emma has locked my post in the van. She knows that there are important documents to deal with before the final hearing. It is just nasty bullying. Go up to see solicitor. Bad fog so stay the night with mum. Miss contact Thursday and contact denied on Friday.

December 15th, Sunday.

When Charlie and Emma return at 8pm Charlie sees me in the kitchen and wants to see me. Emma drags him up the stairs, ranting at me. Charlie in floods of tears. A few moments later Charlie totters down stairs to see me again. Emma rushes downstairs and hauls him up the stairs again so fast that Charlie could not get his feet on the steps. She must really hate me to put Charlie through such treatment so often. What really bugs me is I do not understand why!!!

December 17th, Tuesday.

Go down to collect post, Emma refuses to hand over my post, gets abusive. Mid-morning I ask for my post again. Emma says she is too busy to get it, so I tell her I will get a hammer and break the van window to get it. I go and get a hammer. Emma opens the van and throws my mail into the mud. Emma interrupts the last half an hour of contact, Charlie spends it with Emma. It is so frustrating but still think it is best not to have confrontations in front of Charlie, if possible.

December 18th, Wednesday.

Post locked away again. Charlie with his grandmother. Emma refuses contact, saying it is not worth going to pick him up. Nowadays contact times are changed to suit Emma, I either have to agree or not see Charlie! There is no one to referee this bullying, police are so biased and it takes months to get back to court.

December 19th, Thursday.

Find some withheld mail left on the kitchen table, opened. Annoyed. Emma tells me that she is changing the court order for contact over Christmas, i.e. no contact!

December 22nd, Sunday.

Emma takes dogs and Charlie away for Christmas till 28th.

December 28th, Saturday.

Emma arrives back with Charlie at lunchtime. Two police cars follow her up the drive. Emma kept in dairy by the police for a couple of hours. The police are from the firearms squad. They impound Emma's .38 revolver, kept in the safe. I had referred to it in one of my statements for the final hearing coming up in January. I ask to have Charlie, as per the court contact order. The policeman tells me they had taken him to his grandmother's. He had the gall to tell me that a judge would not want him to interfere. I wish I had told him his job is to uphold court orders. At the time I was too angry to think quickly.

2003

January 3rd, Friday.

Mail still being interfered with, so go to the post office to arrange a PO Box at the local sorting office. Emma tells me to insure the car in my own name and money, and that she has cancelled the standing orders on the joint account. At 2.35pm a court bailiff at the back door summonses me. Emma has made an emergency application (injunction) for occupation of the house and non-molestation orders.

January 6th, Monday.

A lady CAFCASS officer arrives to interview Emma and me (separately). See her during my contact period. Have long phone call with solicitor.

Chapter Six

The Expert Witness

If you are unlucky enough to have to progress through the system, there will probably come a point when you will encounter an expert witness, or indeed have to call on one. It seems to me that once a professional has advised the court in any way, when giving evidence on future occasions, they can then attach the moniker "expert". But this is not a declaration of knowledge or experience as such. When perusing the C.V.s of these professionals you will probably encounter descriptions like "experienced in Public Law cases." Within Family Law there are Public and Private Law cases. Public law cases are where the State is involved, usually through Social Services. These are often cases that involve emergency protection, care and supervision, secure accommodation etc. Private law cases like mine are conducted between individuals and are about residence (custody), contact and parental responsibility.

When I went before senior judges I was surprised to find that they required expert's advice. I expected their level of experience to lessen the need for such experts. I also assumed a degree of training in child psychology or at least a thorough understanding gained over the years. What I found was that there seems to be an unnecessary level of extra cost imposed on the system, bringing in these so called experts, rather than a reliance on a judge's own experience or expertise in Child Matters. Maybe senior judges should be better trained?

The English and Welsh do not have a Bill of Rights or a written constitution. Our laws have evolved out of and with common law—new ones being crafted in Parliament. In our adversarial system laws are interpreted, adapted or amended through the very slow process of appeals up to the highest level, where if successful, they become "precedent".

In the modern era, as society changes at an ever-increasing pace, the law and its interpretation lag far behind. The nation is now a signatory to the European Convention of Human Rights and is no longer sovereign but under the auspices of the European Court. Over time our system will have to merge with the European model, assuming the European Union vision remains intact. At present much of our law is based on the Children's Act of 1989. This applies to children under 18 years of age.

These are some of the experiences I had at the hands of 'expert witnesses'

On an occasion when we went before District Judge Travers, on the first day before lunch we heard evidence from an expert witness, followed by the CAFCASS guardian. In the afternoon the judge decided that the thrust of my ex-wife Emma's argument, that I was a danger to Charlie because I was cruel to animals, was not admissible, as neither expert would agree with Emma that there was any link between cruelty to animals and cruelty to children. Emma's whole argument attested to the understanding that if a person was cruel to animals it automatically followed that they would be cruel to children. This was from some obscure American web site. The judge ordered a recess for Emma's team to discuss whether they wanted to pursue the cruelty angle. When recalled they declined to pursue it. I was called to give evidence. My barrister asked me questions. Then the judge ended the session for the day. In the morning Emma's barrister, a woman, tried hard to get me angry. She bombarded me with questions so fast I could not answer them and got flustered. I could not remember how to properly address Emma's barrister. She was almost shouting at me. So in a raised voice I said "listen lady, slow down". At which point the judge rebuked me for talking improperly to counsel. My barrister thought it was hilarious and said I sounded like a taxi driver getting on his high horse. With the interruption I calmed down after apologising to the court. We were not in the formal court, but what appeared to be like a large office. We sat along a line of tables facing the judge and clerk. He sat behind his own desk. A few times, when I got to the Circuit Court we had the hearings in the old courtrooms. Only twice, over more than 50 hearings, were the barristers and judges wigged and gowned.

This hearing was very important as previously none of the facts and problems had been properly investigated or discussed. He ruled that there was absolutely no reason why there should be any restriction on contact and staying contact should be introduced slowly and expanded till in September I should have Charlie every other weekend from Friday 4.30pm till Sunday 4.30pm. There was not enough time to deal with the exchange arrangements, so he ordered the solicitors to sort something out within a week. He also said he would deal with my problem of getting my possessions back, by correspondence. Emma was refusing to allow me to go to the house to pick them up.

The judge agreed with another of the expert witnesses, the expert psychologist in saying he thought I got angry but did not have an anger problem per se. Likewise he thought Emma was over anxious and would benefit from some treatment. He disagreed with Emma's assertion that I was a danger to Charlie. He spoke at length about his decision to make a "no residency order". He explained that, as Charlie was not living with me part-time he could not grant a shared residency order. He specifically refused to grant Emma residency as he criticised her refusal to observe my parental right to be involved in the big decisions in Charlie's life, such as the choice of nursery; and felt she may be encouraged in her incorrect attitude if he were to grant her residency. The judge had ruled on the first day that there would be no time for witnesses to speak; so they were all sent home. There was no contact for nearly a month after the hearing. Emma vetoed all the child minder options.

In order to get contact restarted on another occasion, the Guardian, arranged for some meetings at his office. Emma took Charlie along to two initial meetings for Charlie to get to know him. Then I was to meet Charlie under the Guardian's supervision in his office the following week. When it came to my meeting, Emma brought Charlie to the office lift, but then took him straight home! No contact. The judge had also ordered that Emma be assessed by an expert psychologist who was to report on Emma's ability to support Charlie's relationship with me.

In the midst of this I met a lovely lady, Karen Brown, and we became close friends. I started to spend some time at her house in London; partly because the driving agency I was working for gave me a lot of work driving lorries in London. Over Christmas and again in the New Year I ended up in the Chelsea and Westminster hospital with problems related to when I had had colon cancer. The stress of the endless court hearings and not seeing Charlie had taken their toll. She was very supportive of my fight to see Charlie and would come down and wait outside during the hearings. She endured my highs and lows, and helped me to relax. When contact was finally restarted her experience as a nanny and her having worked with lots of children in general was very useful and helped me enormously.

During one hearing an expert psychologist gave oral evidence in addition to her report. There was a lot of detail, but the main point was that in her professional opinion Emma was deliberately obstructive about contact, believing that as I had had nothing to do with Charlie's birth, I was not his father and as such I should be dispensed with as soon as possible. Her opinion suggested that Emma's dysfunctional attitudes to men and her relationship with me could be traced back to her mother's influence during her upbringing. She described Emma as very narcissistic. She explained that Emma feared that Charlie's relationship with me would dilute her own relationship with Charlie. The report was 65 pages long and very detailed. In her oral evidence the expert believed that Emma was very unlikely to change her behaviour without a lot of therapy. One of the surprising things to be revealed at the hearing was that at home Emma never referred to me as daddy. I was referred to by my initials, M.R. The judge thought that that in it'self would be enormously undermining of Charlie's relationship with me. Apparently Charlie referred to me as 'Mister' in front of his mother.

The Guardian had also expressed doubts about whether Emma could or would benefit from therapy. He had further doubts as to the impact on Emma if residence was changed and whether she would be able to have beneficial contact with Charlie. He wanted contact restarted, and for Emma to undergo appropriate therapy; but added that if this did not work then changing residence should be considered.

When Emma gave evidence she assured the judge that she had seen the light, and was now converted to the benefits to Charlie and herself of re-establishing a meaningful relationship between Charlie and me. It was just what the judge and the guardian wanted to hear. I did not believe a word of it. Emma agreed to start therapy with someone approved by the expert, and to implement the contact plan. The judge ordered us back for a review. At that time I had not seen Charlie for 15 months. Emma had delayed everything successfully by pure brinkmanship with the judges. When the mood of the court changed to seriously consider the issue of a change of residence, Emma affected a miraculous U turn in court. The judge grasped at that particular straw and adjourned all outstanding issues of costs and the penalty for contempt of court.

At another hearing arranged for a detailed discussion on the expected report on the therapy Emma was to undergo and what progress with contact was being made, Emma had delayed the start of therapy to such an extent that we had to get an emergency hearing to highlight the problem. Contact was progressing as envisaged and going well. Charlie came to London for weekends. He did not like the long journeys, which was not surprising. Emma began to make an issue of this. Finally, and well behind schedule, Emma saw her expert therapist. This left no time for a meaningful report on progress for the hearing later in the month.

Eventually, a year after requesting that the case be moved to the High Court, the judge admitted defeat and let a more senior judge deal with the case. In the two years that he had controlled the case we had not moved on with contact. A more detailed assessment had been made of Emma, but overall we had spent an enormous amount of money with nothing to show for it, except an increase in stress levels. The judge further ordered that Charlie be psychologically assessed and we all had to agree on an expert to assess the likely impact on Charlie of:

1) An order for no contact,
2) An order transferring residence to his father,
3) Contact orders being made within continuing proceedings.

So another year was lost not seeing Charlie.

Adrian Parker, a member of families Need Fathers came with me to the first High Court hearing. He helped me draw up a position statement prior to the hearing. The position statement was drawn up in language that, compared to my barrister's language, was very combative. It was a lot more technical, legal and demanding of the court rather than cooperative. We had to agree an expert child psychologist. Adrian was adamant I had to put forward someone who had experience of dealing with residency change. In his opinion CAFCASS would opt for a pliable psychologist who would deliver the recommendations they wanted. Emma put forward a name that had already been associated with the case, so the judge ruled there was a conflict of interest. When my contender was named, the judge's demeanour changed completely. He became agitated and appeared to be irritated. He looked at Adrian and said he would not allow our choice as he foresaw endless appeals if that expert was commissioned. I was quite taken aback by the adverse reaction of the judge and it made me a bit wary of Adrian's advice and highlighted the problems of getting privately appointed experts. I often felt that senior judges and Cafcass officers should have had the experience to not have to rely on expensive experts to advise. So often the advice was little more than common sense.

On another occasion when the judge gave his opening remarks I was immediately impressed when he addressed Emma directly and said that the courts took a very dim view of any parent that prevented the other parent from having a good relationship with any children. He went on to say that courts took the view that a child benefited enormously from having a loving relationship with both parents. He added that in cases of prolonged obstruction to contact he would have no hesitation in changing residency. Naively, I thought it sounded like he might actually get to grips with our case. I felt quite optimistic. But this was only a directions hearing. The guardian's choice for expert was endorsed. The psychologist was to report on the impact of the three choices outlined earlier. An order was made to observe contact between Charlie and I. Emma insisted it remained chaperoned by her neighbours. There was another order permitting me to have indirect contact by post with Charlie, and Emma assured the court that she would give my letters to my son.

I had brought up the question of continuing or restarting counselling for Charlie at school or privately. The guardian had reported that the school counselling had finished at Easter and that Charlie's behaviour had deteriorated at school again to such an extent that the school had contacted Social Services. Emma suddenly announced that she had already instructed her GP to set up counselling through CAMHS (Child and Adolescent Mental Health Services) and that it was to start imminently. After the hearing I contacted the surgery and they confirmed that they had made a referral but Emma never attended with Charlie. Emma's answer to Charlie's problems was to change school again. Social Services got involved again. In her report the social worker stated that anonymous concerns for Charlie's welfare at home had been passed on from the NSPCC. At the same time the school had reported concerns for Charlie at home from comments Charlie had made to his teachers at school. The concerns appeared to be about Emma's treatment of Charlie, with his mother screaming and yelling at him and locking him in his room. The anonymous caller alleged that the mother's behaviour was becoming worse and unpredictable. I was completely in the dark about all of this till I saw the report in documents before the court from the guardian. Of course Emma accused me of being the anonymous caller to the NSPCC. She and Greg the stockman had fallen out not long before. I would guess that he was either involved or that Emma made the call herself in order to label me as being determined to cause her as much trouble as possible. It was not a serious issue for Social Services as they wrote that no further action was necessary, case closed.

When I had my interview with the expert child psychologist I was over three hours in her office. The next day I was due to have contact with Charlie, supported by the chaperones and observed by the psychologist. The interview was fairly straightforward. She spent most of the interview on the history of my marriage from my perspective. At one point I was quite tearful about all the external pressures on the marriage over the years. I was surprised she asked very few questions about Charlie and myself, or about previous contacts. She said she would invite me back for a follow up interview after the contact. She said I could ask questions then. The contact with Charlie the next day was difficult. The psychologist's idea of observing was to micro-manage the entire contact period. We met at a children's playground. Charlie was not pleased to see me. Eventually we played hide and seek until Charlie came down a long slide. I popped up and said "boo". Charlie burst into tears and ran off. It then started to rain so we all went into a hotel. The psychologist insisted that I sat furthest from Charlie. The conversation was difficult, mainly about school. Charlie's replies were monosyllabic. I had not seen Charlie for over a year, yet the psychologist expected me to maintain a constant dialogue with Charlie who clearly did not want to engage. I had brought some presents that helped break the ice a bit. We then looked through some photos I had brought. Eventually Charlie said he was hungry so I went to buy him some chips. Charlie came to join me in the queue which was an unexpected and very welcome surprise. The psychologist got up to observe. Charlie did not like that so he went back to his seat looking far from pleased. After a difficult period I went off to feed a parking meter. On my return we went to the swings till it rained again. We went into a coffee shop. I persuaded Charlie to play snap. We all played (except the psychologist), and Charlie ended up sitting on the male chaperone's knee. I found this challenging. The whole experience was quite a shock for me. Charlie refused to touch me, let alone kiss me or hug me, or let me hug him. It was the first time I was aware of just how alienated from me he was. A few days later I rang the psychologist's office to arrange the follow up interview. I was told it was not necessary. The psychologist was going to write a report based on that contact as the evidence of the father/son relationship. I had a distinct feeling of a stitch up in the offing.

The psychologist duly produced her expert report of 87 pages. There was an extremely detailed analysis of Charlie. I was struck by the complete lack of any discussion with any person connected with Charlie and me. The psychologist catalogued, in her preamble, hours of interviews with his mother's associates including several neighbours, her so-called partner Alex and Charlie's new school teacher. Given the immediate history of the case I thought it was very odd that she did not speak to anyone from the previous school. She refused further discussion with me. She did not contact any of my support networks that knew Charlie: such as my aunt and uncle, my sister Laurie or Karen.

At the hearing I raised these objections and the psychologist agreed she wanted another observation of contact. I made it very clear that I was not going to be micro-managed in the same way. The judge ordered her again just to observe and not to interfere. The contact venue at a children's Zoo and the arrangements were agreed in court. I was specifically allowed to bring Karen if I chose. At the hearing and in his report before the court the guardian indicated that on-going contact was not a serious option given the history of obstruction by Emma. He had said on balance he thought Charlie would be better off for his long-term development to move to live with me. Because there was only a short time on the day for hearing evidence the psychologist did not express her views. Her report left various options with outline scenarios for each. So the judge ordered a final, final hearing to be heard over three days. He ordered the psychologist to produce an addendum report.

The psychologist changed the venue after the hearing. She overruled all my other suggestions and chose a venue she wanted for the contact. The day before contact her secretary rang to tell me that Karen could not come to the contact. Nevertheless, I arrived the next day with Karen. The psychologist got angry when she saw Karen. She asked Karen to leave and we agreed. I asked the psychologist why Charlie had said he was very concerned about being late back to his mother. When she said she did not know and I suggested she ought to find out why as Charlie had never been late back from a contact. For some reason the psychologist got very agitated and started arguing about Karen not coming on contact again. She seemed unable to accept that we had not objected to her earlier explanation and had already agreed to her demand.

Eventually Karen took charge of the situation, as the psychologist seemed unable to hear or understand anything I said. Karen left and waited in the town for the duration of the contact. The psychologist went on to control and manage the contact session much as she had done on the previous occasion. Charlie was more relaxed this time. The psychologist went on to describe in her addendum report in fairly minute detail every failure of my inability to empathise and connect with Charlie, as she saw it. I made a detailed complaint and rebuttal of most of her points to the guardian and later to the judge. On the contact there were moments when I could discuss things with the psychologist. But overall her attitude came over as "I am the expert, the professional, I question you, and you do not question me!". It is what I call a professional's arrogance. We had a personality clash and I considered her to be hostile. The repercussions in court were to be far more serious.

At the fourth final hearing the positions were laid out by the three barristers, mine, Emma's and Charlie's Then I gave evidence, followed by Emma. We were questioned by each of the barristers, and sometimes the judge would ask questions to clarify a point. For most of the second day the psychologist gave evidence. The judge questioned her at length. She was asked by Emma's barrister to give an assessment of Emma as a mother. She went on to give a glowing tribute of Emma and went further to say that in her professional opinion she entirely believed Emma had had a complete conversion on the importance of good contact for Charlie with his father. She believed Emma would encourage and support such contact. My barrister leapt up to object as the psychologist had not been engaged to offer an expert assessment of Emma. The judge overruled him. She was then asked to comment on the possibility of transfer of residence to the father. The psychologist said I did not have the necessary parenting skills, nor did I have sufficient empathy or put Charlie's needs before my own to permit her to make a recommendation for Charlie to live with me. My barrister objected repeatedly saying that an assessment based on two contacts and one interview was not sufficient for this. But she went on to say that Charlie had indicated that he wished to see his father. The psychologist was confident that contact could be restarted with Charlie's wishes defining contact. She said that Emma had already offered more contacts than her suggestion of 4 short contacts with chaperones in the year. Part way through the psychologist's oral testimony, the guardian's and Charlie's barrister stood up to say that the guardian withdrew his support for a change of residence because he could not go against the psychologist' expert professional opinion. He added that he was sceptical of Emma's conversion, given her history over the duration of the case. The case collapsed.

In his judgement the judge explained that he understood my scepticism of Emma's conversion but agreed with the psychologist that Emma had obviously had a complete change of heart over contact. On that basis he went on to outline the future of contact, expecting the chaperones to be weaned away from contact in three months and that staying contact was to be resumed within a year. He set out an order for a few short contacts and ordered the psychologist, Emma and I to meet again to plan the structure of contact into the future. He also ordered that any deviation from the orders made, including the loss of just one contact would trigger a return to court before him within 7 days of such a notification. He was confident that, as I had demonstrated "the patience of Job" in dealing with this case, I would go along with the process to rebuild my relationship with Charlie. My barrister had been pleased when I had told him we were before the judge, as he described him as one of the golden boys of the system. He had a reputation for getting things done. I was reasonably optimistic that he may be able to control Emma. He had a good control of the proceedings and did not let discussions drift off course.

On another incident concerning the expert psychologist alarm bells began to ring when the psychologist announced that she wanted Charlie to have paramount control of how contact proceeded. To my mind Charlie was completely under his mother's influence and I foresaw Charlie being put under incredible stress to comply with his mother's wishes over his own. The other was the obvious bias from the psychologist. One extraordinary comment by the psychologist during her oral evidence was that she said that what had happened before was no longer relevant to the case. Almost every other expert and professional involved with Emma and Charlie had indicated that Emma did not put Charlie's needs and wants before her own. The judge himself, in his opening remarks had said that the very unusual but obvious observation of the whole case was that from the very beginning Emma had fought over every single area of the divorce. He said it was quite rare for this to happen as most people contended specific areas such as finances. In my evidence I had pointed out that this was Emma's third apparent epiphany, asking why this should be viewed with any more credibility than the previous two? I also pointed out that the guardian had stated in his report before the hearing that he felt contact was not the way forward given the history of the matter. When I left the court on the final day I happened to leave alongside the guardian. He wished me luck with the new orders but he said he knew they would not work and that the expert was completely wrong, Emma had fooled her completely. When I stopped to discuss with my barrister what we could do afterwards, I repeated what the guardian had just told me. In my barrister's opinion the case had been a close run thing until the guardian's position collapsed. He was extremely disappointed with the so called expertise of the guardian, but given his actions in the past he was not surprised that he had taken the opportunity to bottle out (as he put it). He felt that if the guardian had challenged the psychologist' testimony and voiced his opinions, the judge would have listened. That was the guardian's job. In my barrister's opinion this happened all too often with state employed people compared to privately engaged professionals whose next job depended on their reputation. I said I had often complained to Karen that the guardian was more concerned with managing his job rather than doing it as far as Charlie was concerned. At the end of the hearing the guardian asked the judge if he could resign from the case. In the end the judge ruled that the guardian had to stay on but in the role of "keeper of the files". As such he was not expected to do anything. The judge felt that now that Emma had completely changed her attitude he did not feel the guardian had an active role anymore.

After a few days reflection I sought my barrister's advice on appealing the outcome. He said that taking the case to the court of Appeal would be expensive. If I lost I would have to pay, if not all, a high proportion of the costs for everyone else. That scenario would put me into debt. He also said that the appeal judges would most likely support the judge and allow him the latitude to try contact one more time. I dearly wanted to appeal. On the advice I was given, though, the financial risk was too great. At that time I had to subsidise my earnings from my savings to live, so if I got into debt there was no way I would be able to repay it. I had had financial help from my ex-brother-in-law for several hearings up until the third set of final hearings. I felt uncomfortable accepting any further money with no good result to show for it.

So I suppose that my advice would be—beware of the expert witness. Having said that it is not really something that one can have a lot of control over especially those appointed by the other side or by the court. But it is true and should be noted, that as my barrister told me, private expert witnesses have their reputation at stake, and if they can be afforded might be the best way to go. But even that can have its pitfalls it seems as evidenced by the reaction that the judge had to the expert witness suggested by Adrian Parker. Unfortunately this is yet another area in which the courts and the system of justice often fails to deliver.

Chapter Seven

Litigant in Person and McKenzie Friend

In any case that is not funded by legal aid . . . and there is less and less availability for this . . . solicitors are usually the first port of call to conduct litigation on your behalf. They will represent you at court or they might also instruct a barrister to do so. If you decide to conduct your own litigation or represent yourself at court, perhaps because you cannot afford legal representation, you are considered to be a litigant in person.

The court system and its procedures can seem intimidating and incomprehensible; a daunting mass of information, forms, procedure and red tape produced by lawyers and law makers. The justice system, however much it may not look like it, was created for access by the public. All of the information should be available and capable of being understood. And with ever increasing numbers of people who cannot afford legal representation, many are learning to do it for themselves.

Here is a useful quote for anyone thinking of addressing the issue of litigants in person at tribunal hearings. It comes from a case that went on BAILLI, in the Court of Appeal following appeal from an Employment Appeal Tribunal,

DR CLAUDIUS D'SILVA—v—MANCHESTER METROPOLITAN UNIVERSITY

At para. 43, the judgment states:

The other difficulties in the way of a successful bias challenge by Dr D'Silva flow from points made in the appeal tribunal's judgment in the present case. Through no fault of their own, most lay litigants do not have a proper understanding of the legal process, or the way in which tribunal hearings are ordinarily conducted. They will usually be passionately wedded to what they would perceive as the unanswerable rightness of their own case; and many of them will or may regard any and every reaction from the tribunal that they may perceive as questioning their case, or as controlling the manner in which they wish to advance it, as displaying hostility towards the case and bias in favour of the opposite one. In many cases such litigants are merely misreading the perfectly ordinary, and impartial, conduct of a hearing in accordance with well practised procedures.

And another piece published in the Law Gazette 'Litigants in person numbers soar'

www.lawgazette.co.uk/news/litigants-person-numbers-soar
Thursday 13 October 2011 by Eduardo Reyes

The dire state of the economy has already led to a dramatic increase in the number of litigants in person, new figures from a voluntary organisation suggest. This is before government cuts to civil legal aid come into effect, which many solicitors predict will trigger another huge rise.

The Personal Support Unit (PSU), whose volunteers work in courts to provide 'practical and emotional support' to litigants in person, has revealed caseload figures to the Gazette. They show a 19% increase in the eight months to 31 August in cases it supported in the Principal Registry of the Family Division, London's main family court, compared with the previous year.

Cases in the Manchester Civil Justice Centre were up 89% on 2010 in the four months to 30th September. And while the increase at the Royal Courts of Justice (RCJ) was just 5% in the first eight months of this year, this followed a rise of 47% the previous year.

PSU volunteers assisted 6,760 clients with their cases in the accounting year 2010/11.

The unit's director, Judith March, said: 'In the family courts the increase is often recession-related, where clients have either been taken to court because they are unable to meet maintenance payments, or they have gone to court themselves to ask for maintenance payments to be reduced.'

March said budget cuts being absorbed by the courts service had removed many court staff who previously provided basic information to litigants in person: 'At the RCJ there is an entire level of middle management that has been removed.'

The rise in the number of litigants in person is causing concerns about the extra strain placed on the courts system. Writing in the Gazette District Judge Peter Glover noted that the increased burden would inevitably be accompanied by 'significant increases in delay for other court users'. District judges, he warned, are 'nearing the limits of their capacity and inventiveness'.

Litigants in person sometimes achieve dramatic success. Georgina Blackwell a 23-year-old Essex beautician, secured a High Court victory for her mother against house builder Bellway, represented by an eminent barrister, in 2009.

However, Blackwell was not the typical litigant in person helped by PSU. A quarter of PSU clients reported major health problems, often related to stress, anxiety or depression. Over half were from a black and minority ethnic group, and for one-third English was not their first language.

'Many do not cope well with either the written or the spoken word. Many are unable properly to organise their paperwork,' Glover said.

A Civil Justice Council working party will make recommendations to the justice secretary on access to justice for litigants in person by 31st October.

There are many websites and even training courses that you can go on to be LIP but it is not for the faint hearted. It is grueling and draining to do this and for the whole weight of the success or failure of the case to begin and end with your own efforts. I did it for a time but in the end I had to go back to legal representation. I was emotionally and financially drained. After some thought I decided that I could not continue to fight to see Charlie with full legal representation in court. I had approached the senior partner to ask if I could have one of the other solicitors to handle my case. I did not think the one assigned to me was up to the case. However the senior partner was dismissive of my criticisms and ensured me that Ian Hamilton was an excellent solicitor. I had every confidence in my barrister. He was the lynch pin and main advisor in the process. Whenever I asked my solicitor for advice, however, he always had to refer to the barrister or to a senior colleague. My former solicitor, by contrast, rarely had to consult books or colleagues and was always on the ball. However, as far as I knew, you could only get your barrister through your solicitor, so if I changed solicitor I was worried that I may also have lost my barrister. I told my solicitor that I could not afford to carry on. I intended to represent myself as a Litigant In Person (LIP). However Ian Hamilton was keen to pursue an adjourned costs matter. I said I had no confidence that they would be recovered, as Emma always seemed to wriggle out of everything. She always got off scot-free. Ian was adamant that he could eventually recover the costs awarded. It was simply a matter of perseverance. If he was so sure he could get the money, I challenged him, he could put his money where his mouth is and recoup the money with no further expense to me. He agreed that it would cost me nothing as he would just add his costs to the costs awarded to me. So I left him empowered to continue fighting to recover the costs due whilst I would be LIP for everything else. I signed a form to inform the court I would from that point onwards be LIP. At the next hearing the judge again adjourned the outstanding costs issue from previous hearings but ordered that we were at liberty to apply to have it dealt with at another hearing. Ian Hamilton, still engaged just for the costs issue, applied to the court to have it sorted out. As we had come to expect Emma, now LIP herself, refused to supply any information to enable a hearing to be of any use. Finally we had a hearing back before the district judge to have an oral examination of her finances. She had claimed that she could not pay as she was bankrupt. As she was LIP the judge was very patient and explained everything at length and even gave her advice on what to do if she wanted to contest the costs order. She did her tearful "I can't cope with all the extra stress" act, but the judge would not change the substance of the matter. But when we came before our regular judge the following month for contact matters Emma put on a tearful act about the costs matter. Incredibly the judge criticised me for pursuing the matter and said it was another reason that things were so difficult between us and why things were impacting so badly on Charlie. Of course I was not allowed to speak on the subject. I wanted to scream out that it wouldn't have been a problem if he had dealt with the matter properly two years previously. He ordered a stay on the costs.

McKenzie Friend is a term given to a lay person in the court to support a Litigant in Person. The lay person cannot speak or engage in the court process, but may give advice or support like taking notes of the proceedings. An LIP has to ask permission for the McKenzie Friend to be present. Until recently McKenzie Friends were voluntary. Adrian Parker whom I had met through Families Need Fathers and had got himself trained up as a McKenzie friend, outlined what he could do and his hourly rate. His hourly rate was about half my solicitor's. I decided a few sessions might be worth it. By the following January Emma had instructed new solicitors. I was beginning to get cold feet about being LIP at the next hearing. I had my doubts about the aggressive nature of the advice from Adrian, and worried that this might further inflame things. I was also worried about what it was going to cost. He wanted to represent me properly in court like a lawyer, but I decided to use my barrister again. Adrian was very supportive and even much later stayed in contact to see what happened. When I eventually made it clear I could no longer pay for advice he was very generous in giving his time and advice over the phone for free. Towards the end my concerns were no longer financial but rather the impact and effect all this situation was having on Charlie. Adrian opened my eyes to the procedures, protocols and archaic rigidity of the legal system. In many ways he was a breath of fresh air in a regimented and stuffy system. He relished attacking the judges in their lazy, cosy, unaccountable fiefdoms. Before I worked with him I had already perceived that the judges and their attitudes were probably the biggest problem in the justice system's Family Division.

When I re-engaged fully with Ian Hamilton as my child matters solicitor I made it clear that I wanted an economy deal. I was not interested in his attendance at court. In order for my barrister to act for me, he had to be instructed by Ian. I also asked him to keep the other costs issue separate. I could only afford one or two more hearings. I was sent a bill for £11,000 for work Ian had billed to me. This apparently included work on child matters whilst I was LIP. I had a very strained discussion with the senior partner who basically said he knew nothing about any arrangement and I owed the firm £11,000. I explained what the arrangement was, that I had gone LIP and in fact had engaged a McKenzie Friend, whom I had paid. I refused to pay any bills prior to February and expected the firm to honour the arrangement Ian had made to pursue the costs issue at their expense, recouping their expenses when the case was won. In order to reduce costs I had asked Ian to inform the other parties about ending my status as LIP as close to the next hearing as possible. This would mean that Charlie's solicitor would retain responsibility for the court bundle (documents). So all the statements and documents for the hearing had to be filed through them. There is a fair amount of work involved with preparing the bundle for the judge, sometimes other parties object to certain documents being included, so agreements have to be reached. The bundle then has to be indexed so that in court the judge can give a page reference to any particular document to which he is referring. This is all very time consuming. Needless to say Emma's solicitors had an avalanche of correspondence about the bundle. Charlie's solicitor was publicly funded. Extraordinarily Ian Hamilton suddenly was untraceable and uncontactable as my solicitor. In effect he had done a runner! I have read about such things in the newspapers, but did not expect it to ever happen to me. All of a sudden I had no solicitor familiar with my case. Eventually the firm brought in a new lady solicitor. I refused to pay for her to familiarize herself with my case, as she obviously had hours of reading to do so. My relations with the firm were again strained. So my new solicitor did not have management of the case which did save costs. At the final hearing in June 2008 the judge saw no reason for the stay on the costs matter imposed previously to remain. He lifted the stay, making it possible for us to pursue the matter. Emma's solicitors said they were not acting for her in the costs matters. Emma asked for time to seek legal advice. In October I went back to being LIP, except for the costs matter. Whilst I was LIP, I contacted and saw about twenty different firms of solicitors with a view to pursuing the angle of the Clause 8 of the European Convention on Human Rights. Most said I would be wasting my money and it would take years to get to court. One of my interviews was with a very generous lady solicitor. She gave me about three times the free introductory discussion time. She described a case where she had pursued the breach of contact orders with six penal notices till eventually the resident parent was jailed. She thought I should pursue the case getting repeated penal notices till Emma was jailed. I pointed out that Emma already had two penal notices against her and my costs had been more than £200,000. When I asked how much her client had spent, she said “hundreds of thousands of pounds”. I left her office thinking there is something badly wrong with a system that takes a judge to order something six times, and then to have it broken six times, before he did something about it. If you are the non-resident parent and you break a court order without good reason or mitigating circumstances, you are summarily punished by the judge. It seems from my experience and anecdotal evidence that the resident parent (usually the mother) gets away with it time and again.

If you are LIP you need to be good at talking in public, and you need to be assertive with a quick brain. An ability to read legal documents and understand case law at speed is also useful. For someone like me that hates to be reliant on other people the legal system is best avoided. Although I consider myself to be middle class, I acknowledge that my upbringing was in the advantaged spectrum of society. I noticed that the judges I went before were from similar or more advantaged backgrounds. In my childhood the Christian religion was an important element in private school education. We were brought up to view motherhood as portrayed by the Virgin Mary as sacrosanct. I postulate that amongst our judges, and they are overwhelmingly male, there is a cultural bias born of their backgrounds to view motherhood as pure: certainly not evil.

Claiming costs as a Litigant in Person

In civil matters litigants in person can be awarded costs for the work done in connection with their case. The rate is at the time of writing £9.25 per hour. If, however, this does not cover the financial loss for that work a higher figure can be claimed. There is a cap on the amount recoverable of two-thirds of the amount that would have been allowed if the litigant were legally represented. He can also claim his disbursements.

For example, let us say I spent 12 hours preparing my case. He can automatically claim £111 (£9.25 x 12). Let's say that I could have paid a solicitor £3000 to do the work for me. At the discretion of the court, I could claim up to £2000 if I could demonstrate a higher financial loss. Financial losses might include loss of earnings and specific expenses resulting from being a litigant in person.

In criminal matters an acquitted defendant can claim money for expenditure on things like traveling, postage costs, telephone bills and subsistence whilst at court. Rather unfairly, though, they cannot claim for the time spent preparing the case. At the conclusion of the case one should ask for costs from "central funds". Remember, if you go down this route and want to make sure you get as much as you can, you will need to keep receipts as proof of anything that you need to buy.

Marilyn Stowe is a senior partner at Stowe Family Law Firm, and is one of Britain's best known divorce lawyers with clients throughout the country, in Europe, the Far East and the USA. She wrote in her blog recently that:

I have personally encountered many litigants in person who bear a heavy emotional burden. Armed with books and determined to "win", they go into battle like gladiators. The case is all about them, their spouse—hated, with or without good reason in many cases—and their children. What happens in court will affect every member of that family for the rest of their lives. So what can a litigant in person count on? The sympathy of the judge? No. The judge may well give that impression. He or she must be courteous. But a judge adjudicates on law, not sympathy or pity.

I took a straw poll of solicitors in the office, all of whom have had recent experience of litigants in person. Every solicitor had a horror story: from interminable hearings that should have taken minutes, to aggressive misconduct by the litigant, to being wrongly accused of bullying before the judge, to the litigant-in-person's failure to lodge all the requisite documents, or filling them out incorrectly, or refusing to settle on any terms and transforming cases that could have been reasonably conducted and ultimately settled, into stressful, ugly nightmares. The verdict? A resounding thumbs down.

McKenzie Friends

To go along with your efforts as litigant in person, you may want to engage the services of the McKenzie friend that I mentioned earlier in this piece. Anybody can be e.g. a personal friend, a solicitor, a work colleague, or a relative. Anybody you wish who you feel will support you. There is no need for them to be a lawyer. A lawyer can advise you on the law, but you and your McKenzie friend need to focus on the facts of your case. It is the facts you will be presenting and arguing.

Given the limited powers of a McKenzie friend you might wonder why you should have one? Well I would say that as one of the parties in a case, you are, by definition, emotionally involved, and will no doubt have more than a financial stake in the outcome. Emotions can prevent you thinking clearly, listening carefully and understanding what is being said and that is where your McKenzie Friend can keep you focused on the facts, help you present and manage your case in the most effective way, and help you feel less alone.

A summary of what a McKenzie friend can do is basically this:

- Sit beside you in court, which can be a great support.
- Take notes either for action in the proceeding or to look at for future hearings.
- Prompt you to ask any questions that you might need to.
- Keep you focused on your case and on what you want to say.
- Generally be another pair of ears to listen for you.
- Help you stay grounded and keep a check on your emotions and give matter of fact responses.
- Help you to ask questions simply and clearly so they are understood and have the best chance of progressing the case favorably.
- They cannot speak to anybody apart from you.

You will need to tell the clerk at the beginning of your case that you have an assistant who you wish to have sitting beside you. I found my McKenzie friend through the Families Need Fathers organisation but there are other people who are within the area and although not qualified lawyers have a lot of experience in various aspects of law.

If you decide to get a McKenzie friend then these helpful notes from Glen Ferris' website www.mckenzie-friend.co.uk that might give you some information on who to pick as a McKenzie friend.

You need to choose someone with at least the following attributes:

- Calm, collected and politely mannered
- Supportive to you without becoming openly verbal in your defense
- To speak out loud only when spoken to and never at any other time
- Ability to listen and remain focused
- Good note taker, clear handwriting
- Good at understanding written English
- Good at converting your emotional and perhaps biased or initial response into appropriate wording for court use
- Ability to remain utterly quiet during a particularly difficult period in court without rising to your defence
- Able to suggest non legal pointers quietly in court without any disruption
- Willingness to play devils' advocate to help you spot and fix weaknesses in your defence or witness statement.
- Able to do the same for the opposing sides' statements before and during the trial and bring them quietly to your attention

- Someone with a legal background or knowledge of court etiquette would be helpful but not necessary
- Someone who will specifically follow the rules of the trial even if it means sitting passively through what may be outright fabrication
- Possess the ability to accept your decision as final and not argue with you once the session is underway, having agreed the rules of engagement well before the session commences
- The list goes on

There is always a temptation to ask family members or good friends to do this for you and this is great but I would insist you really think about this as they may not be able to contain themselves in the moments when they want to shout out OBJECTION YOUR HONOUR!, or just sit there and stare out one of the prosecution witnesses across the court when they are clearly lying in court. You need someone you can trust implicitly with your evidence, understands the gravity of the situation and can act accordingly and to the guidelines above but most of all and above all else, act in the interests of you!

It should be noted that McKenzie Friends may be liable for any misleading advice given to you, which can mean them possibly being sued by you for the after effects of the wrong advice affecting the outcome of your trial and maybe even the other side for all sorts of reasons! Make sure as far as you can that this does not happen. The last thing you need is further court action!

However, far more realistically, if they stick to the guidelines above and you have a good relationship with them and they are in possession of all the facts available then this should not pose a problem at all and should definitely not put anyone off from doing this very commendable favour.(Also as they are acting in a non-legal manner they are not insured against this type of rare backfire as a solicitor might be i.e. possessing the relevant professional insurance, because of course they are not acting as a professional, they are simply acting as a support / friend.)

It is true that I had not heard of a McKenzie friend before my problems started. The name comes from the name of a case where it was ruled a person going through a court procedure was entitled to have an assistant in court. This assistant can help someone who is representing themselves at court. Although this is very rare there are a few circumstances in which a McKenzie friend is entitled to speak on the litigant's behalf. McKenzie friends have become increasingly popular in recent years. In no way can they replace having a lawyer. In fact most of them are not legally qualified and are not required to be. Some, like Adrian Parker that I was lucky enough to meet are very well equipped but whatever their status a McKenzie friend can be a genuine source of support, confidence and an extra pair of ears in the heat of a court battle.

* * *

Now at the end of 2011 I have woken up to headlines that say;

Family justice review calls for six-month case deadline

The piece on the BBC news website on the 3rd November reports that Children wait on average 13 months for a decision on their case and details an official review that says that Childcare decisions in family courts should be made within six months,.

Former senior civil servant David Norgrove's report said parents should be encouraged to make their own care arrangements when they separate.

The review rules out using the law to give both parents equal access to a child.

A government spokesman said it was vital to "radically reform" the family justice system.

In his report, former senior civil servant David Norgrove said family justice was slow, incoherent and children had to suffer "shocking delays" over decisions about where they would end up.

He said: "Every year 500,000 children and adults are involved in the family justice system. They turn to it at times of great stress and conflict. It must deliver the best possible outcome for all the children and families who use it, because its decisions directly affect the lives and futures of all those involved, and have repercussions for society as a whole."

Mr Norgrove's report said family justice was under huge strain with care cases on average taking more than a year to resolve. Approximately 20,000 children are currently waiting for an outcome.

One of the questions addressed in both Mr Norgrove's interim and final report was whether both parents should have equal rights to access to a child after a separation.

Mr Norgrove did not recommend a legal right in either of his reports, but the interim document had suggested ministers could use legislation to underline "the importance of the child continuing to have a meaningful relationship with both parents, alongside the need to protect the child from harm".

The final report dismisses that idea, saying it could do more harm than good.

But Ken Sanderson, of campaign group Families Need Fathers, said: "The core failing of the current family justice system is that the rights of children to maintain meaningful relationships with both parents, as set out in the UN Convention on the Rights of the Child, are not adequately supported or enforced. By choosing not to address this issue, any other proposals will be merely superficial adjustments to a fundamentally broken system."

The report includes many proposals from the interim document, including creating a single family justice system and making courts focus on where a child goes, rather than spending time looking at the detailed care arrangements.

The review said parents should use mediation and other routes to make arrangements for caring for their children and only turn to the courts as a last resort.

In its first official response to the report, the government said it would introduce a six-month deadline for decisions on the care of children.

"It is vital we radically reform the family justice system to tackle delay and improve the service to children," said a spokesman.

"As set out in the Coalition Programme for Government, this government is committed to encouraging shared parenting and is firmly of the view that children should have meaningful relationships with both parents after separation.

"We will examine carefully the panel's recommendations as part of achieving that commitment."

I see that a lot of the suggestions I have documented as ones that I would think sensible appear in this report but one thing that I find sad and perplexing is the continued bias it seems towards the mother. Why should the father of a child not have a right to see that child once the marriage has broken down? Why is it thought that the mother has the unalienable right to a child and the father does not? Society is always bemoaning the feckless father and the reluctance of many men to take responsibility for their children they sire. Why is it then that when a man does want to step up, to be involved and to be part of a child's life, and even if it seems obvious to everyone that he is an equally good or even the better parent, the bias is always towards the mother? What would a mother have to do for the courts to give a father a chance? Why does it seem that whatever a father does, however suitable, determined and desperate he is to offer his child a loving home for at least part of the time, this so often seems like an unattainable dream that the slightest of protests or lack of cooperation from the mother can so easily derail? And after reports of this ruling today, all I can see is that an impossible situation appears now to be even more hopeless?

This struggle, it seems, is far from over.

Chapter Eight

DIARY

Wednesday 9th July.

Take Charlie down to Laurie's house. The house is being gutted for the builders to renovate. Laurie away. Play on trampoline (boing!), tricycle and in paddling pool. Great day, lots of fun. When I take Charlie back to the farm, Emma is very obnoxious and opens the car door to remove Charlie as soon as I stop the car. I argue that she should wait till I have kissed Charlie goodbye and can hand him over in a civilised way. This is the third time this has happened. Tell her in future I will lock the car and release Charlie when I am ready. But I add that this is not good for Charlie. Emma still going on about Charlie's car seat!

Thursday 31st July.

See new solicitor, for first time properly. Yesterday I saw one of the staff after seeing Charlie. She remembers Greg the stockman boasting about being in prison for GBH.

Friday 1st August.

Go to see Greg's previous employer. She calls him "that bloody thief". Spoke to her daughter at length. Remembered that Greg had said he had been inside for GBH. Good stockman but when the work tailed off he used to leave gates open to make more work for himself, and lots of things went missing. See my hypnotherapist later. She thinks Greg may be a fantasist. His self-esteem is so low that he invents this other violent persona to boost his ego.

Saturday 2nd August.

Pick up Charlie. Emma difficult about the car seat again. So unpleasant, not good in front of Charlie. Have a great day at the park and down at Laurie's. Emma very awkward over sandals I bought for Charlie and she tries to snatch them out of the car. She screams at me about some problem with my new solicitor, but refuses to explain. Charlie is reduced to tears. I bump into one of our associates. She said that she had to see Emma on a Food Links matter. Emma met her half way down the drive, and was so hostile about her writing a letter of support for me that she had to abandon the meeting.

Wednesday 6th August.

Meet the finance barrister at her chambers. Agree to completely new tactics. Abandon Emma's conduct as an issue, concentrate on settlement for £200,000 clean break (47% of valuations). Both critical of previous solicitor's advice and tactics.

Friday 8th August.

Emma's mother Mary changes her will in favour of Charlie.

Saturday 9th August.

Emma so unpleasant we leave as soon as we can. Lovely hot day in paddling pool at Laurie's. 'Boing' popular too! Return in the car with Charlie just wearing his nappy. Emma goes ballistic. Claims her mother is dying. Says she will report me for being a pervert for allowing Charlie to play in the paddling pool with no clothes on! Incredible!

Yesterday had the CSA call to ask about maintenance payments for Charlie. Emma didn't waste any time. Told them that as Emma refused to pay my income from the business I had no money, and in reality Emma had it all anyway. (They couldn't understand that scenario!).

Friday 15th August.

Emma's solicitor rang to say that Mary, Emma's mother, had died on 13th, and Charlie was so upset that he would not be available for contact for some time—a two year old! What bollocks! Had a good session of hypnotherapy. She emphasises that I am a good father and Emma has serious problems. Feel better. Meet one of the farm workers for a drink, says he has had a lot of trouble from Emma and Greg since helping me load up the fridge-freezer.

Wednesday 20th August.

Arrive for contact; a neighbour is there taking dogs for a walk. Emma very pleasant, says Charlie not quite ready, so I say I will wait. 10.20 am Charlie runs out to me. Load pram etc. Pass Charlie to Emma to kiss goodbye. She refuses to take him. She tells me to put him in the car. As I am putting him in the car, Emma snatches Charlie away and storms off to the house. Charlie shouting daddy with his arms out, starts crying. Emma is yelling abuse and shouts "you bastard, why do you treat him like this? You have upset him you nasty man, you're always in denial . . . you shouldn't be allowed to see him at all!" I wait awhile then shout through the back door that if Charlie is not produced straight away, I will ring the police. I ring the police, explain the situation, including reading out the court orders. They will send a car when available. 10 minutes later Emma emerges and puts Charlie in the car seat, kisses him goodbye and tells me to get off her property! I cancel the police car.

I go to the council offices to sort out the council tax summons. It turns out that Emma has paid half of the tax but not passed on the bill to me. I have to pay the surcharge. I tell them I am no longer living there. Charlie is fascinated with the water fountain.

We spent the rest of the day playing in the park. Drive home with Charlie so zonked and exhausted that he was in a deep sleep. Emma accuses me of having done something to him. Over the top! Give Charlie a hug after changing his shoes. Pass him out through my car door—the usual way now. Emma throws three letters into the car and yells that I cannot see Charlie on Saturday. She storms off with no explanation. I read the letters and drive off really mad that nobody can make her behave decently.

Tuesday 26th August.

Jobcentre interview. They have no mechanism to deal with a court order for contact on Wednesdays and Saturdays effectively making me unavailable for work on those days. This exception and allowance can apparently only be permitted if I have a medical condition. The clerk enters that excuse! Can only go for part-time work.

Friday 29th August.

Solicitor rings to say that Emma is applying to limit my contact to half of one day only on the grounds that Charlie is too distressed over contact. He allegedly has disturbed behaviour . . . masturbating and spreading poo over his clothes and around the house. Hearing on Monday.

Saturday 30th August.

Emma keeps me waiting, Charlie waving from his bedroom window. Emma picks a fight over the car seat again, pulls it out of the car. Eventually I ring the police. Emma puts Charlie in the car seat her way, and lets me leave. I cancel the police car.

Monday 1st Sept.

Pre-trial review hearing for finances. Emma is refusing to divulge the contents of the will, so final hearing is postponed. Child matters for Wednesday is adjourned to 19th.

Wednesday 3rd Sept.

Drive down for contact but no one in. Wait an hour. Drive home.

Saturday 6th Sept.

Arrive for contact. Emma is on the warpath. Problems over the car seat again. Emma insists on photographing it. I let her. She then tries to remove the seat, at which point I intervene and step between her and the car. I put Charlie in the seat and buckle him in. Emma tells me to move as she claims she cannot get up. I tell her to use the door to pull herself up. She says she cannot, so I turn and put my hands under her arms to pull her up. She pulls her usual trick and falls sprawling on her back. Charlie starts crying. Emma starts yelling that I always do things in front of Charlie to upset him. I get in the car and drive off without a word: absolutely livid with Emma and myself for falling for it again. I just do not comprehend how she can do these things on purpose so that Charlie is upset. When I return her cousin is with her. Emma gets angry that I keep the car locked until I have changed Charlie's shirt and shoes. Emma is openly abusive in front of her cousin. When I ask if there is any post, Emma slams it down on the car roof. It blows into the long grass.

Tuesday 9th Sept.

Go to see solicitor to finalise statements. Emma has sent a copy of the will, and now demands the sale of the farm and business, with her claim for 60/40. She cannot claim all now that Charlie is to inherit half a million. I am happy to sell everything at 50/50. There is a message that Charlie has a cold so contact is cancelled tomorrow. Final hearing is still to be delayed as Emma is not disclosing the liquid assets in the will (believed to be about £70,000), nor providing accounts for the business.

Saturday 13th Sept.

Emma says I can only see Charlie between 2 to 5.30pm, as he still has a cold. I acquiesce and arrive at 2pm. As I put the pram in the boot, Emma dismantles the car seat and removes a cowboy poncho from underneath. I put the seat back and buckle Charlie in. Emma storms off to the house yelling abuse. I ring the police and lodge a complaint, incident no. 812. They say they cannot get a car to me for a long time. So I drive off to the park. Have fun playing, Charlie discovers sliding down the steep grass slopes on his bottom. Return to the farm, Emma keeps me waiting ages before giving my poncho back. Charlie has no symptoms of a cold!

Wednesday 17th Sept.

Contact denied, apparently Charlie too ill with a cold. Emma says over the phone that the healthcare visitor and the doctor have said that what is going on around Charlie is not good for him. I point out that I hardly see him now. Emma cuts me off.

Friday 19th Sept.

Court day, with barrister. There are 8 cases before the judge. Offer Emma compromise in negotiations, to move back into farmhouse and have frequent shorter contact, she remains living in what is now Charlie's inherited house. Emma suddenly backs out, and we lose our slot before the judge. Go before him at 12.45pm. Emma's barrister really lays it on thick about how difficult I am, and repeatedly refers to the injunction rulings. Judge refuses to consider overnight staying. Adjourn for lunch. After lunch the judge decides to leave contact as it is, except that Emma can swap Saturdays for Fridays unless I get a job that conflicts. Granted permission to have Emma and I psychologically assessed. Final hearing set for 19th December, judge says it is likely the CAFCASS report will not be ready. Importantly the judge said that minor ailments were not a good enough excuse to cancel contact, a doctor's note was required. I drive home ranting at an imaginary judge.

Friday 26th Sept.

Emma still awkward after Wednesday's contact. Emma says that I have to buy my own pram from now on. Charlie is not using nappies so need to get him a potty. Go to Longleat safari park. Charlie loves the monkeys playing on the car, luckily I had removed the wipers!

The highlight was when he was invited in to feed the Siberian Chipmunks from his hand. Delightful!

Really having trouble sleeping—up six or seven times a night. Stress!

Monday 29th Sept.

See the doctor about Charlie and Emma's claims. He seems unaware of most of what Emma says. He suggests that Charlie may benefit from seeing some psychiatric specialist.

Friday 3rd October.

The CAFCASS officer comes to my uncle's house to see me and to assess my uncle's house for future night staying contact. Bring up the idea of applying for residence of Charlie. He shows his bias against young children leaving the mother unless physical abuse is proven in court. He says mental or emotional abuse cannot be proven with one so young. If I want to go that route I will have to start the divorce proceedings all over again from the start. He is easy to talk to and appears to be thorough. Irritated at his bias, but hide my feelings. Miss contact today. Sister Laurie says she can no longer support me financially. Slight panic as to how I am going to pay for the solicitors.

Wednesday 29th October.

Emma says Charlie is too ill for contact and is going to the doctor. Cannot see Charlie for at least a week. Says Charlie is too ill to attend nursery school. I tell her that I have started work on Fridays at a plant nursery. I will need to see Charlie on Saturdays, not Fridays.

Wednesday 5th November.

Have an early hypnotherapy session. Talk about the frustration of the situation. Go to farm to pick up Charlie. Neighbour picking up dogs for a walk. Emma refuses to allow me to see Charlie, too ill. Join neighbour walking the dogs, great to fuss them again. Go to the surgery to check on Charlie's records. Practise manager says she will speak to one of the doctors and she will get back to me. Later she rings me to say that SS has advised her that they should not give me any information. I complain bitterly, and tell her the practice will hear from my solicitor.

Wednesday 12th November.

Refused contact on last Saturday. Arrive to pick up Charlie as neighbour collects dogs for walk. Emma pleasant, but does not produce Charlie till we are alone. Charlie lets out an enormous yell "daddy" and runs over as fast as his little legs will carry him. I agree to return Charlie early at 4pm so that Emma can take him to carnival later. On return Emma says I cannot have Charlie on Saturday as she has no proof that I have a job. Emma has recently changed solicitors and the new ones refuse to act for her until her public funding certificate is transferred. She refuses to see the contract, saying it has to be sent to her solicitors. I get the contract copied in town and go back and leave a copy in her post box and send a copy to her solicitors. I go round to the nursery and speak to the nursery owner. She checks her records and confirms that Charlie has not missed any days recently. Charlie now does Monday, Tuesday and Thursday mornings.

Had a good 'Families Need Fathers' meeting in the evening in Farnham.

Wednesday 19th November.

Emma very aggressive at pick up. Refuses to look at job contract. Tell her I have sent copy to her solicitors. She demands that Charlie is returned at 4pm as it gets dark. I tell her we will be back at normal time. Cold, blustery day. Quite difficult to find warm shelter for contact. Meet CAFCASS officer for him to observe contact. In the evening Emma rings to demand to know what Charlie ate during the day. She claims Charlie has been violently ill since his return. Told her Charlie ate very little for lunch. Suspect this is a set up.

Saturday 22nd November.

Can't sleep, so drive down very early to see Charlie. Everything looks normal at farm at 9am. Go and have a cup of tea in town. Return at 10 am. No-one about. Just driving out of drive at 11.07am when Emma appears in the van. Drive back up the drive behind her. She rushes over to the back door to unlock it, then back to Charlie's door of the van. I get out of my car and lock the doors as I have my papers inside. I walk round to Charlie's side of the van. Emma has the door open, backs and turns and when she sees me she belligerently asks what I am doing here. I reply "for contact, as per the court order!" She argues that I cannot see Charlie as nothing has been decided. I tell her that I have a job on Fridays and she has been advised that I will be seeing Charlie on Saturdays. She has had ample time and opportunity to see the papers, but has refused to do so. Whilst talking I get up close to the open door and manage to get between Emma and Charlie. Emma gets quite heated and tries to pull me away. I try to unbuckle Charlie's seat belts. I yell at Emma to stop. I turn round and push her away. She loses her footing on the pile of scalpings and stumbles over to the corner of the building with her right hand out. She continued into the wheelie-bin and fell over it. The seat belts are caught up. Emma comes back really angry, pummelled my back and grabbed my arm and pulled me away. We tussle back and forth. Charlie bursts into tears. We both call each other names and things get heated. I say I will call the police and they can come and sort it out. I manage to dial 999 as Emma tries to grab the phone out of my hands. When I get through she starts screaming to the police to come and save her son! I can hardly hear a word for all the screaming. I say we will have to wait for the police to arrive. She keeps attacking me and pulling me. At one point I raise my fist and yell at her to back off or I will hit her hard and it will bloody well hurt! She ignores my threat, and continues to try to pull me away. I close the van door. When she next pulls me hard, I turned and step towards her. She loses her balance on the pile of scalpings and as she goes down she puts her right hand down into the scalpings. As she falls her left hand skids across the gravel. We were still yelling at each other. When she gets up with a look of pure hatred she says "I am going to get an order to have you locked up, and you are not going to come near me, and when this is over you are never going to see Charlie again". She tries repeatedly to get to Charlie's door handle, but I stand in the way. She says she needs to let the dogs out through the sliding door. I tell her use the rear doors. She didn't.

We calm down, but we still set to over certain things. She says I am mental. I say she is sick and needs treatment and that she is just like her mother, who was really sick and evil. She counters by saying I lie, so I challenge her to name one lie. She can't. She repeatedly says I am not Charlie's dad. Charlie has quietened and is sucking his thumb looking at me.

The police arrive about 20 minutes after the call. Emma immediately starts to cry and sob that they must save her son from me. She is taken inside by a PC while I talk to a sergeant. I take Charlie out of the van and cuddle him. We go into the utility room and I give a brief account of the episode. I show him the court orders and contract letter and two payslips from the plant nursery. They get confirmation of the court orders via the radio. I am left with Charlie for a while and we laugh and joke and cuddle. The coppers returned and say they were duty bound to arrest me as Emma has a graze on her left hand. I exclaim that I had phoned them because *she* kept attacking *me*! They take me to the police station. After emptying my pockets and signing papers I am put in a cell. The duty solicitor arrives at about 3pm and we talk. I get tearful at the end at sheer frustration with the law. I am fingerprinted, charged with common assault and told to attend the magistrate's court at 9.45am on Thursday. I drive to a lay-by and write this whilst still fresh.

Thursday 27th November.

I arrive early for the court. I am only one in a suit, most are young men in track suits. Go in to court 1, called to the dock. Give name, address and date of birth. Asked for plea. Not guilty. Given bail to remain. Have to wait hours for the trial date as Emma's witness, the PC, has to agree date to attend. Eventually sign a blue form, back before Magistrate to be told to appear on 12th Jan. Ask if contact is to continue. Told it will be dealt with in civil court later.

Wednesday 10th December.

Pre-trial review hearing before a judge with a terrible stammer. First encounter with Emma's new solicitor, who is a very aggressive, rude, scruffy, fat unpleasant woman. Judge agrees I have a right to a hearing to discuss contact, as waiting till mid-January would be detrimental for Charlie. Emma solicitor will not speak to mine! Hearing set for next Wednesday.

Wednesday 17th December.

Come off night shift at the hotel and drive down for contact hearing. Go before a lady judge, in the new crown courts. Very plush! My solicitor negotiates for ages with Emma's barrister. Emma produces a very long daily log of alleged behaviour by Charlie supposed to show the effect of contact on his behaviour. New tack. Emma argues that nursery is Charlie's refuge and cannot be used for contact exchange.

Judge asks what is the alternative? Emma says there isn't one. Judge says "nursery it is then!" Nursery not open on Saturdays so only have Wednesdays sorted. Make a complaint that CAFCASS officer did not attend as ordered. Judge ordered that arrangements be made for Emma and I to be assessed by a psychologist as soon as possible. Earmarked final hearing sometime in April CAFCASS report has to be filed for court. I call in on the mechanic and tell him what Emma has said he had said about Charlie with me. He is angry that she had not asked him first and said it was not true!

Friday 19th December.

Finances Final hearing. Meet my solicitor and barrister. I tell them that Emma will do everything to avoid selling the farmhouse. She can push Emma to the limit. They want to negotiate. In November Emma had changed tack and decided she did not want to sell the farm. This caught me out as I had agreed to a very low valuation that I thought was irrelevant, as the farm would be sold. I ran up a bill with the solicitors of over £1,000 just arguing over the valuation, largely because the valuer had not put a value on the new dairy building. It had cost over £70,000 to build. Emma offers a very low pay-off and wants nominal maintenance. (This means she can come back to court later to renegotiate!). I refuse and tell the usher I want the judge to decide. Emma comes back with more serious offers.

Eventually offers £195,000 and clean break. I tell my solicitor to hold out for £200,000 (49%). After a wait, Emma agrees. Now we have to negotiate the possessions. Emma slowly gives up her demands. My solicitor really worried that I am pushing too far and says to agree so the whole deal doesn't unravel. I tell her to hold fast. At 4pm Emma agrees. The usher is anxious as the judge has dealt with everyone else and is waiting to go home. We spend ages drawing up the 7-page order so that Emma cannot wriggle out of the agreement. Eventually we sign the document with the usher flapping around chivvying us along. We go before the judge, he signs it and the deal is done. Solicitor advises that I should now apply for legal aid as if I am going forward on child matters alone I will never have to repay, whereas Emma is on legal aid but as she has fought finances as well she will have to pay it back or have a charge on her property. What a weird system! Emma will now come after me for the Injunction hearing costs too, 75%.

Feels good—the first victory!

Tuesday 23rd December.

Pick Charlie up at nursery. He is a bit taken aback when he sees me across the room, then lets out a yell and barges through the other kids to leap into my arms. The nursery owner says it is so good to see him so happy. We spend much of the day at Court farm. The farmer comes in with a bottle to feed the orphan lambs and asks if any of the children want to help. Charlie gets agitated, and says "there's a man!" He then says he doesn't like men. I ask him if he likes daddy. “Oh yes” he says. I ask her if mummy said she didn’t like men, “yes,” he said.

Saturday 27th December.

Pick up Charlie from Emma’s cousins house where they have been for Christmas, drive back. Have a wonderful day meeting many of the family and giving him Christmas presents. He was amazingly easy with so many strangers and was a delight. He even ate well. No sign of behavioural problems.

Wednesday 31st December.

Go to pick up Charlie. Charlie very chatty all day. He plays with his cousin happily and seems to get on well. Charlie is so zonked at the end he sleeps all the way back and doesn’t really wake up properly at the house.

Saturday 10th January 2004

Contact at the contact centre 2.30-4.30pm. Arrive to find Emma already there with Charlie. I wait in a large room with other dads seeing their kids. Charlie brought through so I do not have contact with Emma. (Good). There are four elderly supervisors who spend much of their time clucking around the children. Charlie is not at ease. He wants to kick a football around outside. We have to be supervised, like we are criminals. Charlie sees Emma sitting in her van and is distracted, keeps asking why mummy is there. When I go to get the football, one of the staff insists on accompanying me! As we sit cuddling near the end, a woman keeps coming up to tell Charlie to play with the toys. The whole place gives the wrong impression to Charlie, and is very intrusive. I ask to take Charlie for a walk, but I am not allowed to leave the premises with him. I tell them that it was supposed to be just an exchange venue. Also told they are not open regular days, as they are staffed by volunteers. On the drive home I decide not to see Charlie with such limitations in future. As the psychologist said it feeds Emma's paranoia that I am dangerous and she will tell Charlie that I must be dangerous if contact has to be supervised.

Monday 12th January.

Meet counsel, (very young) at the Magistrates Court. We are second trial today. She confers with the crown Prosecutor, who says the case should be dealt with in the civil court. He suggests that I be bound over to keep the peace. Counsel explains that if I keep the peace for the time limit I will have no criminal record. If I fail to keep the peace I will face a new full trial, loaded against me. I say I am happy as long as I am considered not guilty. The case will be dismissed. He spends ages trying to persuade Emma to go along with this. She wants a full trial. He thinks it unlikely she will get a conviction, so do the deal. I go into court no.1. When the chair magistrate comes in and sees me, he walks straight back out again. He was my old homoeopathic vet! So after a delay I am ushered into court no 2, before a lady chair. (Three lay magistrates sit). I stand in the dock as the lady reads out and explains about being bound over for 6 months (the minimum) for £50. Afterwards the Crown Prosecutor passes and stops to thank me for a very honest statement, repeating again that he was irritated that the matter had not been dealt with in the District court.

I go to Charlie's surgery to talk to the doctor about a copy of the records for court, and see our farm worker about being a witness, probably in April.

Drive home and go off on night shift at the Hotel.

Wednesday 14th January.

Finish night shift at 7.30am and after a quick breakfast dash down to see Charlie for contact. Only on Wednesdays now. Weather cold and wet but we manage. Play at the park, then go down to Laurie's house. Drive home very tired and tearful. He is such a poppet. Once a week is not enough, but I will have to make do somehow.

Saturday 6th March.

Drive down for assessment by the psychologist. Three hours of mainly questionnaires, and a discussion at the end. Seemed to concentrate on my old fashioned attitudes to parenting and anger issues.

Wednesday 10th March.

The psychologist comes to observe contact with Charlie at Laurie's house. She stays about 2 hours. She declined to join us for lunch, where Charlie played up a bit as he wanted to sit on my lap. Played on the 'boing' afterwards. The psychologist said she has seen enough and added that Charlie was obviously enjoying himself. She left. We had a fun day playing. I send my wage slips to the CSA to prove earnings.

Monday 15th march.

The CAFCASS officer comes to see me at home, straight after night shift. He asks about the Magistrate's court decision. He is hostile, and says that Emma has already told him that I had been found guilty of assault. I suggest that he contact the court. I give an account of the incident. He says Emma is going to pursue it in the 'Child Matters' and had shown him photos of bruising all over her body. He thought things should be left to settle down. I say this is unlikely to happen with Emma.

Wednesday 31st March.

Didn't see Charlie last week, as he was ill. The CAFCASS officer comes to observe Charlie at Laurie's house for about an hour. He says he is going to see Charlie at home to see what he is like, following Emma's complaints that Charlie is manic after contact.

Wednesday 14th April.

Last time to pick up from the nursery. Emma has refused to allow it again following the owner providing proof that Emma had lied about Charlie being too ill to see me or to attend nursery back in November. Charlie sang Old Macdonald has a farm repeatedly as he has just learnt it at nursery! Good day at the zoo.

Receive the psychologists' report—a whitewash, waste of £2,000.

26th/27th April.

Final hearing about contact for Charlie. The judge asks the psychologist to speak first, followed by The CAFCASS officer. Judge tells Emma's team that their submission about cruelty to animals will not be accepted as an argument. I am questioned. On the Tuesday Emma's lady barrister who is very aggressive, fires questions rapidly and is almost yelling at me. I get flustered and can't remember how to address her formally. I get ticked off by the judge for saying, "listen lady, slow down!" Emma is questioned, by her counsel. The judge is quite shocked by Emma's answer to the question:

"How important is it for Charlie to see his father?"

Answer: "About as important as playing with his peers at nursery."

After lunch the judge sums up and then constructs the order. Exchange arrangements not resolved. Judge tells us to sort it by next week. Witnesses were sent home early as the judge said there would be no time to hear them.

Saturday 21st May.

First time I see Charlie in over a month. Emma delayed contact as she insisted on being present at exchange in a child-minder's house. Eventually all child minders back off saying they are uncomfortable with Emma. One said Emma threatened her. The judge agrees to interim handovers at the farm gate and I agree as long as Greg is not present. Pick Charlie up at farm gate but Greg is there too. Nothing said. Have a great day down at Laurie's on our own. Laurie on holiday in France. Charlie said he was upset that he had not seen me for so long. Exchange back at farm gate. Leave Charlie to walk over to Greg. His car is parked across the entrance to the drive. Emma is waiting in her van 5 yards behind. Not a word said!

Friday 18th June.

Join a Father's 4 Justice march in London, ending in front of Downing street. About 2500 all dressed in some purple. Fun, light hearted march, police laughing along with us. Crowds come out at Trafalgar square to cheer. Hear some sad stories.

Monday 28th June.

In court for contact breaches before the judge. Wait till after lunch to go before judge. He is in wet mode and refuses to address any of the problems. We are told to recess to find an exchange venue. Emma eventually agrees to a local nursery if I pay all the expenses. (We should have started staying contact after the last hearing in April). Judge refuses to address the problems about collecting my possessions from the house. He says Emma can stay, but neither she nor Greg to be present. Agree to neighbour observing. He refuses a costs application because he says Emma starts off obstructively but has become amenable . . . only because we bring her back to court! Can't believe how naïve he is, or is it prejudice? The judge leaves at 4pm, and we run out of time to scrutinise the order being drawn up. Ushers ask us to leave as I point out that the "no residence" order has been left off. What a shambles! Underhand tactics to frustrate the proceedings by Emma's legal team.

Saturday 3rd July.

Off down to have contact with Charlie. Pick up at the nursery. Great not to see Emma, as we are separated by 15 minutes. Charlie overjoyed to see me and the nursery owner asks me for a coffee to chat. Although very showery, we spend lots of time on the 'boing' and slide at Laurie's. Charlie zonked on the journey back and is still sleepy when I say goodbye. Tearful journey home as I fear this kind of pattern of long periods not seeing him is on the cards.

Saturday 11th July.

Laurie and I go together to pick up Charlie from the farm gate. Greg is again there. The nursery owner is on holiday. Have a good day at Laurie's with mum. Charlie accepts that he has another grandma and likes the attention from Laurie and grandma.

Saturday 17th July.

Pick up Charlie from the nursery at 1pm for first STAYING contact. Drive back and on the journey Charlie announces that I am a nasty man and he should not be seeing me. And that mummy will find him a nice daddy. I keep my cool and ignore the comments. Halfway home he gets out of his seat and comes and stands behind my seat. He leans over and hugs me round the neck and showers me with kisses. I say I like hugs and kisses; he says he does too and Mummy likes them too. Charlie had a cold swim in the pool and then he had a late birthday cake. In compliance with the court order he had to talk to Emma on the phone at 6 pm. He answered a litany of questions about what he had done so far! I read a story till he fell asleep. He woke at 4.30am and cried for mummy. He quietened when I eventually asked if he wanted to get into my bed and have a cuddle. (Charlie says he still sleeps with mother much of the time). What do you do? I had bought him his own trampoline for his birthday, so we set it up and played on his new 'boing' between the showers. Grandma comes for lunch. Charlie is so tired from the 'boing' that he falls asleep on my lap before pudding. As the nursery is not open on Sundays, we arrange to return Charlie to the neighbour's, at 5pm. I had a memorable weekend. Charlie is well worth fighting for, I only hope I don't let him down. Off to the Hotel for night shift on return.

My solicitor starts maternity leave.

Saturday 31st July.

Down to see Charlie for day contact 10-4.30. Pick up from the neighbours. Good fun in the park and then up to the Zoo. Charlie says that mummy doesn't like me and that I had hit mummy. (Apparently my initials M. R. have now apparently evolved into 'mister' I am never referred to as daddy). He says mummy hits him when she is cross and hits the dogs. The cat has gone because mummy got cross when it got into the van. Charlie has an accidental pee on the zoo climbing frame. Change in the disabled loos. Back in time to the nursery.

Charlie asks if I am a nasty man, so I ask what he thinks. After some thought he says he doesn't think so. He asks the question a lot when we are driving anywhere, so this has become a useful time for us to talk things over.

Saturday 7th August.

Pick Charlie up at 1pm for 2nd staying contact. Lots of swimming and "boing". Big scare over getting a hornet stuck in his hair. The slapping the hornet out of his hair upset him most, but he was not stung. After a cry and cuddles he is back to normal. Grandma comes to lunch on Sunday. Charlie sleeps like a log through to 8am! Back to the neighbours' for exchange. Everyone on tenterhooks at the Hotel as the chairman is staying for a few days. Otherwise boring night-shift.

Saturday 14th August.

Pick up Charlie for a day contact. Go to Monkey world, near Dorchester. Charlie loves it; he even did the long slide that was scary! He was very concerned about the one-armed gibbon, especially when the keeper said a cruel man had hacked it off when the gibbon was a baby.

Sunday 15th August.

Drive down to the farm in a van to collect my furniture. Arrive at 10.15am to find Emma and Greg and a neighbour waiting. Emma is very aggressive and orders me about. Obviously not afraid of me when it suits her! It started to rain. All my stuff was in the garage, away from the house in part of the dairy building. I tell Emma that the court order specifically states that she and Greg must not be present, but can remain in the house. She will not listen, so eventually I ring the police. They arrive 30 minutes later. After reading the orders they tell Emma and Greg to go. They stay to watch the loading till they get called away. I get more wound up as it becomes obvious that some things are not present, many things are deliberately damaged and some things were substituted for more inferior things. The worst was the maze of deep scratches on the dining room table.

The strimmer was present but with none of the attachments, so it was useless. The chainsaw had the choke mechanism broken off, immobilising it. My radio was substituted for an old one of Emma's mother's that did not work. She did not miss a trick. In the beginning I had explained that I would have nothing to do with Greg, under any circumstances. I said he was a lying cunt, and I was sick of his perjury. I was so angry with him after all I had done for him, that I actually used the C word. Our neighbour had been in the navy for 20 years plus, so he had heard a lot worse. I took the stuff down to one of Laurie's barns, and took the van back and drove back. Then went to the Hotel for the night shift, and then back home for a quick breakfast and then off to the plant nursery, mowing all day.

Saturday, 28th August.

Pick up Charlie for w/e. His cousins are staying too. Spend time in the pool. Charlie eventually plucks up courage to jump in from the side, and then won't stop. He is a plucky little swimmer! The kids play together most of the time, with play-dough and colouring books. Charlie enjoys the alpacas and his 'boing'.

Sunday, 29th August.

At 4 am Charlie gets into my bed and then sleeps through till 8 am. He says he still sleeps with mummy mostly. I disapprove, but no point in saying anything. My uncle and aunt fly off to Spain. When I drop Charlie back at the neighbours they say they can only do one hand-over a month. I wondered how long it would be till Emma found a way to scupper my contact. For a 2-hour journey, it took 9 hours to return via the A303 because of the holiday w/e. Luckily I am not on at the Hotel tonight. I am irritated that I have to do all the journeys and pay all the expenses of handovers.

W/e September 11th/12th.

Pick Charlie up from the nursery. Have a great w/e playing on his 'boing' and feeding the Alpacas. Lots of visitors in and out of the house. Return Charlie to the farm where Greg is waiting. Dash back to the Hotel for night shift.

Saturday 25th September.

Drive down to pick up Charlie from the nursery. A mile from the house the nursery owner rings to tell me Emma has cancelled the contact. She invites me in for a chat and coffee. I explain that yesterday Emma had asked that I forego the next contact as Charlie had a party on Saturday morning. I had suggested that I pick up Charlie from the party venue. For reasons unknown this was not acceptable, and after further argument I agreed to forego the day for Charlie to go to his party. (There was still no other exchange for Sundays, except the one Sunday a month at the neighbours.) I presume that Emma has denied contact today so that I will not see Charlie for over a month. I am really pissed off and frustrated that she can repeatedly get away with this behaviour.

Saturday 2nd October

No contact, Charlie goes to his friend's party.

W/e 9th/10th October

Pick up Charlie from his nursery. Stop at Tesco with Charlie. At the check-out he suddenly asks why I hit mummy. A lot of people's ears prick up. I patiently explain that I have never hit his mother, but that he saw me pushing mummy away when *she* was hitting *me.* Charlie is very clingy all day. He insists on watching the Jungle book DVD. Fun with the 'boing' and alpacas. He crawls into my bed at 4.30am. So when he is asleep I slip into his bed. He wakes at 8.45am (brilliant) and is indignant that I swapped beds. I tell him it was time he slept through on his own. We go to the Apple Festival at Blackmoor. Charlie enjoys the bouncy castle and the pet's corner. Charlie is very shy at lunch with the other visitors. After lunch he wanders out by the pool. He trips on one of the pool cover straps and falls onto the pool cover that is over the pool. We all joke that '*he has fallen in the water'* as per the Goon joke. (Obviously he did not fall in the water). We drive back to the farm, to be met by Greg blocking the drive with his car. A new barn is being constructed close to the entrance. This is puzzling as Emma maintains that she has no money. I am concerned that Emma has purloined Charlie's inheritance (£70,000 in liquid assets) for this. Charlie will need all his money for a good education.

Tuesday 19th October.

Finish working for the Hotel. Work full time for the nursery for the same rate of pay. Emma refuses to allow further contact as she is adamant that Charlie says he fell in the swimming pool on the last contact. We have a court day booked for 17th November, so I just have to wait for a judge to sort it out. She doesn't miss a trick!

Saturday 13th November

Help man a stall for Fathers4Justice in Portsmouth High Street for a few hours. A surprising number of the public voice their support.

Wednesday, 17th November.

In court. I arrive late as M4 closed from an accident. Barristers try to negotiate, but I refuse to give up any contact time, especially staying. Go before the judge. Emma very uptight, glaring at me. The judge refuses to change or vary the order, save having two single Saturdays to start. He grants me staying contact from 28th to the 1st January. Great! The judge is taken aback by Emma's aggressive argument that she should not have to share the journeys. He orders her to do half! Both barristers ask that in future either a Circuit or High court judge hear the case. I ask the judge to order that Greg is not to be present at hand-over. He agrees.

Saturday 20th November.

Drive down to pick up Charlie for the day contact. No-one around. Call in on the nursery to pay the bill. No contact.

Saturday 27th November.

Drive down to pick up Charlie for the day. Greg has blocked the drive again. He is unpleasant and tries to wind me up while I wait for Emma to bring Charlie down the drive. I have objected to his presence as he seems determined to incite me to a reaction. Charlie runs over. We go to the park and then down to Laurie's. On the way Charlie says that he would chop me up in two pieces and eat me, and then he will get a nice daddy. Poor kid is very troubled! We had a good day playing and then watched Bambi. Charlie got quite upset that Bambi's mother got shot and that the hounds attacked Bambi's friend. On the way home I ring Emma to tell her I will not do the hand-over at the farm, but would meet her at the supermarket car park in town. I feel safer in a public place. She was so unpleasant on the phone that I have to cut her off. We wait at the entrance to the store. Emma drives in with Greg in the van. We return to the car, and I lock us in when I see Greg come over. He walks around my car, and as he comes level with my window he becomes extremely abusive, but in a low voice. I tell him that he was not allowed to be present and that I want nothing to do with him. He told me to fuck off repeatedly. I call the police and explain what is happening and that I feared an incident. Towards the end of the call Emma appears in my headlight. Greg backs off. I give a running commentary to the police. I let Charlie out of the car to go to his mother. I apologise to the police controller and ring off. I do not say a word to Emma, and drive off.

Friday 3rd December

Finish at the plant nursery at midday. Drive down to pick Charlie up from supermarket car park. Emma comes with a neighbour in the car, but Greg is parked two rows back in his own car. Exchange and we drive down to Cornwall to stay with old friends from college days.

The next morning Charlie proudly announces to everyone that he slept all night in his own bed. We went to Hollywell bay and messed about on the sandy beach and dunes. He seems at ease with strangers and is tired out with all the attention from my friends' much older children. He sleeps like a log all night. On Sunday we do a tour of my friends' strawberry farm. He is happy to be carried by Jeremy for much of the time. After lunch we drive back and Emma comes with Greg again to pick him up from the store car park.

Monday 6th December.

I go to the doctor. I am so stressed out, exhausted and sleeping really badly that he signs me off work for a week.

Friday 17th December.

Solicitor rings in the morning to tell me that Emma is refusing any further contact until at least next June/July. This is to give Charlie time to have counselling to overcome the trauma of contact. I would laugh if I were not so angry! My solicitor says he will get an emergency hearing to deal with the loss of Christmas holiday contact. So, no contact.

Solicitor thinks we should make an ex parte application to have a Penal Notice attached to the order. The thinking is that if Emma carries on like this much more, the judge will send Charlie to live with me. We should start thinking about applying for change of residence.

Thursday 23rd December.

Drive down for emergency hearing before Circuit judge. The last slot before closing for Xmas break. Judge is irritated by Emma's barrister, who attempts to prolong things on a technicality. He orders a recess to sort out Xmas contact between ourselves. Emma refuses. Judge is further annoyed and tells us to return after lunch, when he has sorted the other cases out. Later we had the hilarious scene where the judge says that he expected his order to be obeyed. Three times Emma's council has to say that Emma would not obey. The judge even addresses Emma directly. His expression when Emma basically tells him to get stuffed was memorable. He makes all sorts of threats, including the possibility that he could order Charlie to live with me. He could give a suspended sentence, as had the judge, two weeks earlier. He is inconsistent as he then refuses to impose a Penal Notice as he expected Emma to obey his order, (even though she had just told him she would not!) My solicitor tells me I have to go down on the 28th for the contact with a witness, in case there was no contact.

Wednesday 28th December.

Drive down to pick up Charlie. No one around. Wait an hour, drive home. No contact!

Chapter Nine

What was the point?

What is the purpose of the civil court? Most people would probably say that it is to deliver justice. This would certainly be the case if you were applying to the civil court for redress for some harmful action against you. The Family Court, however, is totally different. At my second hearing, before the only lady judge I encountered in my fifty odd appearances in court, I was without any hint of irony told that the court had nothing to do with justice: it was all to do with the interests of the child. That raises some interesting questions. First, civil courts were invented to referee disputes to prevent violence being the final arbiter. If basic justice is not part of the final solution then the solution will not be satisfactory. Secondly, the court is there for solving disputes where one side refuses to negotiate. It should, therefore ensure that parties to a negotiation or settlement stick to their obligations. Sadly the Family Court fails on both points. On the point of natural justice, historically in Victorian times, women had no rights over their children in a marriage. Indeed in extreme cases husbands had their wives committed to asylums if they did not obey their demands. Now we have the situation where the pendulum has swung too far in favour of mothers' rights. Because of the basic injustice in the system, fathers have now had to find their voice to call for a change to a more balanced system. The Family Court also fails abysmally on how to deal effectively with mothers that are serially in contempt of court. It is pointless having a system that judges refuse to enforce. What really angered me was the assertion that prison was the only sanction, which was not to be used as it was against the child's interests to be separated from the mother. In rearing children there is a concept called "tough love". Sometimes the child has to suffer in the short-term for the greater benefits in the long term. Take an extreme case of abuse of children, when they are used as child beggars. Rarely do the Police deal with this effectively, claiming that to send the mothers to jail would not be good for the children. So the mothers are at best warned, but they are not deterred and soon return to using their children to beg. If mothers were prosecuted for child abuse, the children would at least get a start at schooling while they were in care. Education is the route out of poverty. If the policy was one of zero tolerance, the attitude of mothers to child begging would change. The point is that if judges attach penal notices to orders and then do not enforce them, they destroy the belief in and respect for the rule of law.

Judges are presumably amongst the most intelligent strata in society. Why then are they so pathetic at identifying other punishments. That is what they have been trained and are paid handsomely to do; to apply their knowledge of the law to engender a solution to an intractable problem? If mothers have money they can be fined. If they live on benefits, they could possibly be withheld for a period. In cases like mine, where another housing solution was clearly available the mother could be ordered out of the family home for a while to let the father live there to start rebuilding a relationship, with least disruption for the child. It would deliver a message to the mother that the court could not be manipulated. In so many cases the mothers apply for and get benefits from the state. I see no reason why the state should not expect compliance with the rule of law, and should withdraw benefits temporarily as a punitive measure. If the child was deemed to be at risk then the child should be sent to stay with the father temporarily or, as a last resort, taken into care.

These measures are about tough love and refusing to allow mothers to hide behind and manipulate the children against the father or indeed the court. The damage to my child by being brought up by such an abusive mother without any balance from the father's influence will be far more devastating on my child's life than six months of turmoil followed by a balanced and settled normal home life. Because my case ran and ran with no sanctions ever being applied to the abusive mother, I ended up wasting most of my money to pay for the legal farce. It is certainly not in the child's interests to have either one or both parents so financially exhausted or destroyed that the state ends up supporting them. The child will obviously have less opportunity available to him or her if the parents have no money left.

Another argument that irked me was when a judge would say that it was not in the child's interests to be moved from the family home. When I was a child many of my peers' parents were in the Armed Forces. It was not uncommon for them to move house every two years. It was not ideal, but the important point was that the child saw both parents. In my own case my parents divorced when I was thirteen. I spent the rest of my childhood between two very different homes in the holidays and enjoyed both.

I have heard very senior judges say that punishment for contempt of court is very difficult and complicated. It is not; it just takes the will to deal with it. I left the system after eight years when I realised that the senior judges who held my fate in their hands were lazy, somewhat incompetent and complacent. There is a commonly held belief amongst fathers and father's support groups that the senior judges obfuscate and procrastinate in the expectation that fathers will walk away either through frustration or because they have simply run out of money. What really upset me was the hypocrisy of tough talking judges and their constant assurances of full support for help in maintaining contact between father and child, and for dealing with the obstructive mother—that came to nothing. It is a great shame these feckless judges cannot be sued, or at least named and shamed, in the system for their behaviour; now that would be justice! I am still unsure whether this was down to prejudice, incompetence or bias or a combination of those. For judges to claim they have no powers is disingenuous. The consequences of my injunction hearings were that I was ordered out of my house, removed from my business and eventually forced to sell it to my wife for £1. They took away my house, job, company and in effect my child with their orders. If they could do this to me, why was it that they could not do anything to make my ex-wife comply with the orders they placed on her?

Of course we all know that when rules or laws are broken and no sanction is applied, it is tantamount to a green light to a miscreant. My child's mother is very sharp and soon got the message. Three times at three different points in the long struggle she claimed to have seen the benefits of contact for our child with me and promised the court to completely reverse her obstructive attitude and positively encourage and foster a relationship between my son and I. Being generous I can, in retrospect just about accept two of those conversions. But I find the third claimed conversion, given her resistance over every aspect of child matters and finances, to be one too many for the judges and certainly me, to believe. It would have been useful to have an ombudsman, unconnected with the Judiciary that I could have asked to review the case.

When institutions carry out their business behind closed doors, we inevitably find cover-ups, incompetence and just plain sloppy, lazy decision making. One improvement to the Family Court process would be independent ombudsmen that could be called in to examine the course of a case and have the power to publically criticise judges for their decisions if they are feckless. Because the process is at present behind closed doors and secret till my child is eighteen, the judges escape criticism. I have an overwhelming sense of complacency in the Family Court. People have called for serious reform for years but little progress has ever been made. I see no reason why judges as well as lawyers could not be annually assessed on their results in court, possibly being weighted for their years of experience. A league table, not unlike those for schools, could give an indication of competence and achievement. Of course, like the school league tables, they are not the complete answer, but they would stir up the complacent and add a measure of competition to a virtually stagnant profession. A consequence I would hope for would be that lawyers became more combative with judges and complained about feckless judges holding up cases.

Judges interpret the law and instigate government policy; defined by laws made in Parliament and the emphasis put on them by ministers. Today government policy is woefully muddled about the role of fathers in the family and in society. On the one hand government declares that family is the bedrock of our society. Government asserts that it is really important, vital even, that fathers have a meaningful role in the rearing of their children, not least in providing financial support rather than leaving the state to pick up the tab. We are told of a growing group of single mothers in society that in successive generations in each family have had no male or father role models, and are entirely dependent on state benefits. It appears to be a self-perpetuating phenomenon. We have the Child Support Agency that is designed to go after fatherhood deniers to support their offspring. There is little help or even sympathy for those fathers that are denied access to their children and who then retaliate by refusing to support their offspring financially. The CSA is not interested in the reasons why.

On the other hand, we have government policy that encourages the notion that fathers are now irrelevant. When my wife and I sought fertility treatment it was only available either on the NHS or privately if you were in a long-term relationship with a partner or spouse. Now single women, and presumably men, can apply to have a baby by artificial means. The family unit is no longer obligatory or apparently upheld. No doubt if that option had been available to my wife years ago, she would have taken it and not had had to marry me to have children. It is just confusing for government ministers to bemoan the existence of these dependent single mother families and yet openly encourage the pathway to such situations.

The world has moved on. Many people consider the greatest threat to our civilisation is the overall warming of our planet, and in particular the element of that warming that can be attributed to human activity. The human activity component of global warming will never be contained with a growing world population and increasing spread of wealth. That combination drives global warming. So why do we have such an irresponsible policy to encourage single parents to have children? There is a valid argument that the state should not be financing fertility treatments at all. Why does the government not take the lead and restrict family/child benefit to the first two children born to either man or woman in a relationship? The parents would then have to assume financial responsibility for any further children.

I had been brought up with the imperial spin that, like most things British, our courts and justice system were the best in the world. This was a message further reinforced during my education in the private school system where it was continuously drummed into me that the British value of fairness was one of our most famous national characteristics. If it was not fair, it was not cricket.

Even when I myself was caught up in the legal system, for a long time, I clung to the unreal expectation that the great British justice system would prevail and everything would come right in the end, after all the goodie always won, didn't he? When I became a member of Families Need Fathers I began to get a sense of the anger and frustration that so many fathers felt at the apparent lack of basic justice in the system. In the fathers4justice meetings I met some men whose anger and bitterness was consuming them—one or two trying hard but not really succeeding to hide an undertone of violence. Every so often the media reports horrific cases where fathers who have been denied proper contact or, in their eyes, have not been able to have enough contact, take extreme action and kill themselves and their children. I do not condone such actions, who could? But I now have a better understanding of how these tragic situations can occur, how frustration and sadness, grief and anger can eat away at you.

The biggest injustice, however, in the family legal system is that people known as 'parents' collectively, when considered separately as men and women are not considered emotionally or in any other way equal. I have encountered this prejudice repeatedly. When it comes to raw emotions we are still animals. In nature there are two dominant emotions, to procreate and to protect our young. The way our society has progressed or evolved for men at least, it has long been ingrained into us that we should not show any emotional weaknesses to those outside the family, in case those weaknesses should be exploited. It is perfectly acceptable for women to show their emotions in our society in all and any situation. I appreciate that in my lifetime many of these norms are being overturned and many men are experiencing some confusion over this. It is also a given that most fathers are not as eloquent or can rarely deliver with powerful emotion a description of their emotional links with their children in the same way that mothers seem able to do.

One of the biggest things to affect me in this whole process has been depression. For a long time I was unaware that I was suffering from depression. I have always made a conscious effort not to brood on matters, but it is inevitable to some extent. I sought a lot of treatment and counselling so I assumed I was coping quite well. But depression affects people differently. For me my IBS condition can have me up several times a night depending on the stress levels. After waking for the second time in a night I often found my brain would go into overdrive and I would find it difficult to get back to sleep. I would often have imaginary rants at judges in the early hours. Whether this was helpful in processing my anger and frustration at these feckless individuals, I am not sure. When I was working for the driving agency I found sleep deprivation to be a real problem.

After I had decided to back off from seeing my child I had a period when I was not sure I was doing the right thing. I would lie awake for ages debating with myself. One of the important reasons behind my decision to be self-employed was so that I could regulate my work to fit my sleep needs. I did not have to start at a fixed time in the morning, and if I needed to sleep in till nine in the morning I could do that. I have found this flexibility has helped my ability to deal with depression, as I often found myself in a downward spiral largely due to lack of sleep. I have also found that now that I am no longer entangled with my toxic ex-wife I have risen out of the low mood phase. One consequence I did not expect to find is that I am not driven to build my new business in the same way that I used to be. I used to work very hard, but now I lack the drive. It has been suggested to me that as I had everything taken away from me, I am subconsciously fearful of a repeat scenario and thus temper my drive to be successful again. It may simply be that I do not have a passion for the work I do now in the same way as I did for livestock farming.

There are times when I feel I shall always suffer from some melancholy. My child is not dead so I cannot grieve. I pass a school or see something on the television that pops a memory of him into my head, closely followed by the confused emotions of sadness, loss, perplexity, anger and frustration. The longer the separation goes on, the more pronounced the emotion because I know it is unjust: neither my child nor I have done anything wrong to deserve such cruelty and torture. There are obviously distressing times like birthdays and Christmases that cannot be avoided. I have to learn to cover the emotional loss or face the well-intentioned encouragement from those close to me. This usually just magnifies the predicament and accompanying emotions. Unlike grief it is not an emotion that I can share with anyone close; they have no connection with the turmoil that I feel. The usual but incredibly irritating response from strangers is that when my child is an adult he may come to look for me. Without a childhood in which to form that trust and bond, the adult relationship is unlikely to be so deep. And there will be no memories to recall.

One of the things that being shut out of his childhood has prevented, and this perturbs me greatly, is that now I wonder how I can now let my child know of his origins as a donated embryo in our fertility treatment. During the course of the treatment my wife and I attended the obligatory counselling. Following strong advice from the counsellor we discussed that advice and agreed to tell our son of his origins somewhere between the ages of six to nine. We were told that the earlier the better was best for children as they grow up with expanding knowledge and understanding to accept their situation. This is preferable to being told as older children or adults when it will come as more of a shock, very often leading to bitter resentment at not having been told earlier. This is not information that can be given in a letter. It requires sensitivity and support at the time and afterwards. Now that his mother denies any agreement to tell Charlie it seems that I am unable to do so, because I do not see him. Although Emma has been quick to tell Charlie from a young age that I am not his father, I am not sure he understands. Of course Emma makes no mention of her similar biological status. The fact that we are legally, but not genetically or biologically Charlie's parents, will be very important at some point in Charlie's life. Not least as he almost certainly has siblings and will want to know his genetic health projections, as he gets older. I am frustrated that I am unable to manage the situation as I would like and I fully expect that this will all end in tears one day.

I have never been happy taking medication or drugs. My alternative to anti-depressants is to go walking. Because of my health condition walking also aids my body to absorb water better, so I have less problems with dehydration. I believe most forms of exercise release feel good chemicals into the body that improve mood. When I was a student between retraining courses I took five weeks off to walk the pilgrimage route “Camino Frances” from the French side of the Pyrenees to Santiago de Compostella and on to Finisterra on the Atlantic coast of Spain: a distance of about 500 miles. I met many wonderful people along the way, but also spent, by choice, time walking on my own. You have the discipline of walking for much of the day but the freedom from normal pressures to explore your thoughts, feelings and desires as you walk. You have the time and space to review your life and where you want it to go. Along the way the scenery, cultural history and people lift your mood and encourage your mental exploration. For me it was a profound experience but I was not really aware of the full impact till after I got home.

Many friends have suggested that I try meditation as an aid to de-stressing and keeping calm. I have not found it easy and probably not tried hard enough. I have found that to go wildlife watching is akin to meditation for me. I focus all my senses and direct them at particular things. It clears my mind of everyday thoughts and stresses. It works for me. I have often wondered if fishing has a similar effect for its devotees.

When the idea of changing residence became a serious option Emma was repeatedly questioned by barristers, judges and experts and asked to explain how she would feel if Charlie was taken away from her. Her consistent reply was that it was so inconceivable a prospect that she could not even acknowledge it, let alone quantify her feelings about it.

Nobody ever asked me what I felt like being prevented from seeing my son.

At one hearing as we finished a discussion about a possible change of residence the judge demonstrated his prejudice by closing the hearing and saying that as I had not produced a detailed plan for how I was going to look after Charlie, he was going to adjourn the case. I had been given no instruction before the hearing that I should produce such a plan. Secondly he could have spent ten minutes questioning me as to what I intended if he was really interested. And then, when at later hearings I produced such a plan—he never referred to it.

A child expert psychologist had been given three options to consider for the court about Charlie having a relationship with me. One of the options was to change residence; the expert was to ascertain the effect that would have on Emma and on Charlie. She conspicuously failed to address any of this in her report. It became obvious from her oral examination in court that she had never intended for this to be an option. As I explained earlier she also failed to interview any of my supporting friends or my partner to explore my emotional links with Charlie. The overriding impression I got in court was that as a father I was perceived as having less emotion invested in Charlie than his mother. I am not saying I felt the same as Emma, because I recognise that men and women feel differently about things. What I resent deeply is that I was automatically considered a second-class parent on account of my gender. On the few occasions that Emma or I spoke in court, when the subject of a change in residence came up, Emma would, without fail, put on a great emotional act with tears and sobs. These always made the judge uncomfortable. These 'tantrums' usually produced a pithy comment from my legal team. On one occasion the guardian leant across and said "Oscar performance this time!"

As a continuous and monotonous backdrop to my whole legal experience, I spent hours waiting in court anterooms before going before various judges at the County Courts. To relieve the tedium on occasions my barrister would explain the workings of the system. I was rather disconcerted to hear him describe the guidance of a case as being like a giant game of chess. It was important to know in advance what was likely to happen and what was likely to be said. He would, for example, never ask a question to which he did not already know the answer. It always seemed to me to be very wasteful of time in court when we could easily have written detailed statements for viewing beforehand. As things stand most of the time in court will be spent reiterating the substance of those statements, with the other side trying to trip you up or catch you out. Of course for most of the hearings Emma and I never said a word. I would guess that to be a barrister you would have to be in the top 10% of the population academically and intellectually. Plainly barristers are not stupid. Judges are selected from barristers. That's not to say, however, that in my experience, several judges were not foolish! My own barrister hoped one day to join the Bench. I came to the conclusion that barristers wanting to be promoted to the ranks of judges are not likely to criticise the body they want to join, in public. One criticism aired occasionally was that having spent years as barristers meeting and dealing with the worst side of divorce and warring parents, when elevated to the Bench much of that insight apparently and inexplicably disappeared. When we discussed why, I learnt that part of the problem lies in how judges are promoted. It was explained to me that the measure of a judge's success was the number of appeals against him; the fewer the better for his or her promotion prospects. I would have thought a measure of success would be how fast a judge successfully dealt with a case. The longer a case runs the more expensive and intractable it becomes: by any measure less successful. The penny dropped! I understood why our judge endlessly adjourned my case with review after review instead of dealing robustly with it. It also explains the great reluctance of most judges to transfer residence, because it is such an emotive order that it is likely to be appealed. The system actually rewards judges that obfuscate and procrastinate. In my case a different judge did eventually get the measure of the problem. If Emma's bad behaviour had been dealt with properly early on, the situation would not have gotten so out of hand with Charlie ending up being so emotionally abused by his mother. If Emma had been dealt with properly or even, as a last resort, harshly by going to prison or being made to pay for the endless review hearings, then she may have appealed. If the appeal judge upheld her complaint then it would have affected the original judge's promotional prospects. This is a system the machinations of which cause the presumably unintended consequence of prolonging cases and causing more collateral damage to children in the long run.

I complained time and again about our original judge's attitude to costs. His favourite escape clause for my case was "it is not in the best interests of the child". In my case Charlie had inherited far more than Emma and I from our share of the divorce settlement. If Emma had been ordered to pay the costs of the hearings brought back to court because she had broken the latest contact order, then there could have been two consequences. First the financial pressure could have curbed Emma's behaviour, or secondly she would have carried on till her finances required her to sell the farm. In which case she could have moved into Charlie's inherited house two miles away. The judge said it was not in Charlie's best interests to be moved from the family home.

At what point does incompetence become prejudice?

I was advised that if Emma was eventually proven to be guilty of breaking the contacts then I would be able to recoup most if not all of the costs to that date. As it was she was found guilty of contempt of court, she appealed and lost. After that the judge went out of his way to shield her from paying any of the costs except for two small hearings. He then aided her in avoiding paying those costs for years. His prejudice over the costs debacle was extraordinary. He was the major cause of my second great complaint of the system. Why should I have to loose £200,000 in my fight to see my son when I had done nothing wrong? And yet Emma was found guilty and criticised by nearly every professional involved with the case and suffered no penalty at all. Was this British justice?

I take issue with those judges that constantly hide behind and use the excuse that their decision not to take any definitive action is because it is not in the interests of the child. In Article 8 of the European Convention of Human Rights, it states, amongst other things, that everyone has the right to respect for their family life. The courts have taken the view that while a balance must be struck between the competing interests of parents and children, the welfare principle continues to predominate under the Children's Act 1989. Predominate does not mean to exclude. Several judges appeared to refuse to deal with situations where they criticised Emma for doing something wrong but then declined to do anything, claiming it was not in Charlie's interest. The attitude over the family home is a case in point. Where Charlie lives, as the guardian told me, was irrelevant as long as his basic needs were met. In my case Charlie even had his own house, where he had spent weeks living with his mother. Time and again decisions were made which were blatantly biased in support of Emma and by default thwarting me, in the status quo.

I listened to an interview on the radio with Mrs Hodge, a minister in the labour government. For much of the interview she vehemently denied that there was any bias in the Family courts against fathers, or more particularly non-resident parents (nearly always fathers). I listened with incredulity, wondering which planet she lived on. The spin was pretty relentless.

I found the most marked difference in the use of judge's powers to intervene. In the injunction hearings the judge used some pretty draconian powers against me. I had admitted on three or four occasions that I had retaliated to Emma's storm of harassment. This is typically where the law is an ass. My admission of a few instances of harassment compared to the daily barrage I was subjected to by Emma, meant I was the guilty one. I continued to deny the finding that I had interfered with the business. But the judge found for Emma in these things. His response was to order me out of the family home and impose an exclusion zone, despite the fact that he was made aware that it would be very difficult for me to maintain contact with Charlie if he did this. I was also ordered to sell my half of our company to Emma for £1. In effect I was ordered to leave my home, sell my company, resign my job and give up my lifestyle choice to be a farmer. In short I was ordered to give up everything I held dear in my life. Even in the most acrimonious divorce very few men lose their jobs too. Most men are able to keep that anchor in their lives. The fact that Emma had already gone to live with her mother two miles away was immaterial. He could have ordered her to live with her mother who was dying, and where she was to spend much of her time anyway. Yet when it came to child matters and enforcing contact orders, the judges claimed they had little power. I think a more accurate description would be that they had little ability to make a useful decision; or in plain English, they were feckless!

Over the years my legal team put forward many ideas to help resolve the contact problems. I do not remember any being accepted or implemented. Emma seemed to have the power of veto over most things. The modifying influence on Emma's behaviour was the threat to move Charlie to live with me, and she usually presented good behaviour and reconciliatory advances just before upcoming hearings when she perceived this as a genuine threat. When the judge removed that threat, Emma continued to frustrate contact by endlessly delaying procedures and intimidating the guardian.

The higher up the court ladder we progressed the more the judges exclaimed they had more options to deal with the problems. A High

Court judge in particular said several times there was more he could do to help sort the problems. But they never put forward any new ideas. They seemed wedded to the idea of contact, even though the history of the case demonstrated such problems. Towards the end of the process I put forward some ideas. The judge had said it was important to rebuild my relationship with Charlie but for him staying away from home was too stressful. I suggested that he order Emma out of the house for the summer holidays and the following term. I could then move in and live with Charlie. He would rebuild his relationship with me, whilst keeping his familiar surroundings and friends.

It would shock Emma into realising that the court was serious and if, after this period, things did not improve then Charlie could be moved to live permanently with me. This and more unconventional ideas were not even acknowledged by the judge. Eventually I wrote and told him I was out of ideas and asked if from his experience of cases like mine, he would put forward something useful. Although he often claimed to have other options, he never put any forward. I found this two-faced attitude from the judges, where they would say one thing and do another, very undermining of any respect they might expect for their status.

I sought advice from all sorts of quarters. I saw an advisor from the Citizen's Advice Bureau who happened to be a barrister. The conversation wandered into the area of the European Convention and Court of Human Rights. I pursued advice from charities like Liberty and the Aire Centre in London. Liberty said it was not their kind of case. I got good initial contact with the Aire Centre, but my case handler left to go and work for another employer and as I result I lost continuity and eventually contact with the charity.

As I have said earlier whilst I was litigant in person (LIP) I saw about twenty different firms of solicitors with a view to pursuing the angle of Clause 8 of the European Convention on Human Rights. Most said I would be wasting my money and it would take years to even get to court. One of my interviews was with a very generous lady solicitor in Bognor Regis. She gave me about three times the free introductory discussion time. She described a case where she had pursued breach of contact orders with six penal notices till eventually the resident parent was jailed. She thought I should pursue the case getting repeated penal notices till Emma was jailed. I pointed out that Emma already had two penal notices against her and that my costs had so far been more than £200,000. When I asked how much her client had spent, she said "hundreds of thousands of pounds". I left her office thinking that there was something badly wrong with a system that took a judge to order something six times and to have it broken six times, before he did something about it. If you were the non-resident parent and you broke a court order without good reason or mitigating circumstances, you would be summarily punished by the judge. It seems from my experience and anecdotal evidence that the resident parent (mother) got away with it time and again.

The same attitude pervades the police. Whenever Emma broke the contact order I was ordered to leave and take the matter back to court. I was told by the police that if I did something wrong I would be arrested. On the matter of allegations of domestic violence, I well remember the senior police sergeant telling me that I could not win in those situations. I would have to actively avoid them or suffer the consequences. It was obvious that the court, using the precautionary principle, viewed me as guilty or at best suspect until I proved myself innocent.

When it became a matter for consideration, comment and then analysis by professionals no such reciprocal principle for Emma's emotional abuse was deemed necessary. Even the judge's explicit denunciation of Emma demonizing me in Charlie's eyes did not elicit any limiting steps. Even though Emma had had two previous 'conversions' from her negative attitude to Charlie having a relationship with me, the judge grasped the third 'epiphany' wholeheartedly without any precautionary principle applied. I found it irritating not to mention expensive that early in the divorce proceedings Emma could make an allegation of domestic violence or abuse that after months was found to be groundless. She could then go ahead and make another allegation and we would go through the whole lengthy process again. What surprised me was that there was no financial penalty for her making untrue allegations and wasting the court's time. On the other hand, I had to pay all my costs to fight the endless string of allegations. In my opinion the courts should allow only one hearing for such allegations, and then if this allegation is found to be baseless, for any further allegations the person making the accusations should be made to pay all the court hearing costs. This I believe would be a powerful deterrent to those that just want to delay proceedings or smear their opponent.

One of my most serious criticisms of the system is the time it takes to do anything. I believe that there are critical periods in a child's development that the courts should do their best to accommodate. These periods revolve around education. The first and most serious is when the child starts formal school aged 5. In my case the court was aware there were problems from the time that Charlie was 15 months old. By the time Charlie was two years old the court was well informed of the contact problems. The judge had detailed what the problems were before Charlie was 3 years old. If the case is to be handled robustly, it is best that is done before the child starts school. If, as in my case, the parents live far apart, before a child starts school is the best time to try the more extreme remedies like longer staying periods or even residence change. The other periods where undue stress for the child should be avoided is in the run up to important educational goals like GCSEs and A levels. One of the major reasons for not seeing Charlie now is to give him some stability and peace at school. It is tragic that Emma moved him from his school again, causing more upheaval for Charlie. The judges should expedite the course of a case to these ends. Where there are children of mixed ages this is obviously not so practical.

It is true that children are resilient. My own parents separated when I was 12 years old. I learned quickly to adapt to the two different households and two lifestyles; one in a town, the other on a farm. One area I was initially very ignorant and naïve about was the impact on very young children's patterns of behaviour and attitudes to life: the earlier the experience, the more ingrained they may be. I know nothing of the training judges receive, but from what I gleaned from the attitude of the judges I went before, I doubt whether they bothered to study much about the psychological importance of the experiences a person was subjected to in their life; especially that laid down in the earliest years. Some say that your life patterns are laid down or learnt by the age of one and a half years. The Jesuits claimed that if they had a child for the first seven years of its life they could influence that person for life. From what I have learned from counsellors, psychologists and therapists in general and from what I have belatedly read, the kind of behaviour she exhibited and what Emma was saying to Charlie before the age of two will have made an irreparable impact and have enormous repercussions on Charlie throughout his life. It is child abuse!

I am struck by my experience with Emma. I feel that senior judges should undergo some degree of training in psychology, so that it is not necessary to have so many experts in court. It would be cheaper to train experienced judges rather than use publically funded experts.

When Emma's mother disowned her, Emma seemed genuinely shocked and distressed by the experience. When we began to get an inkling of what her mother had done and said to Emma after walking out on Emma's father, Emma seemed genuine in her assertion that she would never do that to me nor treat a child so abominably. Yet when she became pregnant she appeared to morph into a clone of her mother. With the benefit of hindsight it is now apparent to me that after Charlie was born Emma became overtaken or possessed by the effect of the grooming or indoctrination her mother had drummed into her when she was a very young child. It seemed as though she was unable to override this learned behaviour. Had the seventeen or eighteen years of our marriage been just a sham? Was it simply that when Emma finally got the prize she had strived so long for, a child, a switch went on in her head and the childhood learned behaviour surfaced? Emma is not stupid and can follow all the arguments and criticisms of her behaviour by the court and its hired professionals: and yet she remains in complete denial of her behaviour. I have struggled to understand how that could be. I have often heard it said that if you repeat a lie often enough you begin to believe it. Yet it remains puzzling, and to some extent scary, that Emma attended therapy, albeit under duress from the court, and emerged saying what people wanted to hear but remained fundamentally in denial and unrepentant. The psychological assessment of Emma concluded that she was anxious; she claimed to be afraid of me and afraid of what I would do to Charlie. One thing I am certain of is that Emma has never been frightened of me. She attacked me physically at least seven times in our marriage. I defended myself by leaving the scene, which invariably made her even angrier; I never hit nor hurt Emma in anger. She has made it plain since our separation that she thinks I am weak and pathetic. I realised after a while that Emma expected me to give up and leave them alone. If I had known then what I know now, I would have walked away, saving myself from financial ruin and being emotionally hung, drawn and quartered by the experience of having my son legally kidnapped and groomed to hate me.

Emma has never had any cause or reason to accuse me of doing any harm to Charlie. Charlie was never late back from contact with me. I never received any complaint, nor did the court, for any injury sustained by my son during our contact sessions. Allegations were made but they were never specific, always vague and unable to be confirmed by any professional. Even the allegations that Charlie was sick after contact and had nightmares were never corroborated by anyone else. When professionals were engaged to look out for these things or visit the house after contact, they could find no evidence to support Emma's concerns and allegations.

In the 50 odd hearings I had in my struggle to see my son, I went before 16 different judges. I was, as I have said, brought up to view judges with respect and as pillars of our society, almost beyond reproach. By the end of my involvement with the courts I am sorry to say that that respect has evaporated. That is not to say that they are not honest, decent people, I am sure they are. When you consider that they are drawn from the more successful barristers, why do they, once they take that seat on the bench, become like timid old ladies? In a fit of pique after one hearing I rounded on my barrister and exclaimed, "why is it that when judges leave home in the morning do they leave their balls behind?" My barrister expressed some sympathy with my view and opined that he had noticed that even the most vociferous, passionate barristers became timid on the bench. He thought there was a culture of "don't rock the boat" amongst judges.

My biggest criticism of judges at important hearings was their unabashed use of hollow words. Many times I heard and was heartened by strong words from the judge laying down the law and saying that they would deal sternly with miscreants, and warning in the most sombre tones that the courts were not to be ignored. But these were, it became apparent, hollow words. Time and again the judges failed to remonstrate with Emma for her behaviour. She soon learnt that she could get away with anything. The only judge to read the riot act was the lady judge, but unfortunately she never sat for any of the more important hearings. The only judge who commanded a vestige of respect from me was one at an injunction hearing. Although I did not agree with much of his judgement and much of it was flawed, he took some bold decisions.

Most judges declared that they would do what they could to improve the situation for Charlie. I was particularly disappointed by one judge's decision to close the case without even consulting me. It demonstrated to me that after assuring my team and me that there were things he could do if contact did not work, all he really wanted was to get rid of the case at the earliest opportunity. He chose to ignore all my concerns at the last hearing I attended before him. When, several days later, I told him I had taken the initiative and stopped contact because of the cruel and damaging effect it was having on Charlie, his earlier sentiments about having other ways to sort the problems seemed, once again, to be hollow words. I got heartily sick of hearing judges say to Emma that they took a dim view of her obstruction to Charlie and my contact and that if it continued they would deal with her. It was a commonly aired view at father's support group meetings that many judges prolong the cases by doing nothing so that eventually the father gives up. If any domestic violence was admitted then the advice was not to bother going for contact through the courts, as you would not stand a chance. I wish that either the way judges are promoted could be changed or that they were paid in line with results. Perhaps if they stood to be awarded a bonus if cases were resolved with a good ending quickly with correspondingly reduced pay for cases that dragged on or ended unsatisfactorily, attitudes would change. It reminds me of a conversation I had with my father after a couple of years of litigation. His opinion was that the courts rarely solve anything but that they soon parted you from your money. He said that even Mrs Thatcher, who took on the unions, would not take on the judges. They have too many friends in parliament to allow for any serious reform to be a possibility. At the time I thought his view was rather jaded. I am not so sure anymore. For some reason the thought of turkeys voting for Christmas comes to mind!

Something that has always struck me as odd and extremely unhelpful in the court process is that once a judge has made an order, for example for costs, he does not then follow it through and see that it is obeyed within a certain time limit. It would be simple for the clerk to confirm compliance with the appropriate legal team. But no, bizarrely it is up to the opposition to pursue it often at further cost and time. This automatically makes the atmosphere between the two warring parents even worse. It should not even have to be dealt with in another hearing, but by correspondence. Judges it seems have no responsibility to follow up or ensure compliance with their orders! It would be hard to invent a more dysfunctional system than that which we have in place.

What I would favour would be a system of mediators with the power of a judge to intervene and who would have the power to order reports from any experts necessary for a case. The mediators would see the parents for child matters only. There would be no legal representation allowed except for parents with handicapped intellect or poor communication skills. The rough outline would have a morning or afternoon per family once a month. Initially meetings would be with each parent separately and then together. The mediator would stay with the case. A good mediator would get to the bottom of the problems, face-to-face, fairly quickly. Cafcass or similar organisations could be engaged to report on schools and housing arrangements etc. These reports could be graded for useful detail and paid for to reflect that grade. In the vast majority of cases the problems would be identified within 6 months or 6 sessions. Each session would be recorded and the mediator would keep a file of notes and reports. One of the big problems with the law dealing with family matters is that one size does not fit all. With our open society and different types of parental partnerships case law is not suitable and should not apply. At present the law is only changed if a successful appeal is made at the highest level. The judges at the highest level are elderly and generally out of step with modern Britain. In essence the law does not adapt quickly.

The government need only to give the broadest of outlines of the basic principles for child matters. The rest could be for the mediator and parents to agree. What one couple agrees to does not have to apply to others. The system would do away with legal aid. Orders from the mediator would be written on the spot for each couple, to be shown to police or other agencies as necessary by a parent.

The whole system would be simpler, cheaper, quicker and fairer and above all not so confrontational. Both parents would be continually consulted. The present system has many parallels with the NHS dealing with psychologically based illness. The judge is like a doctor who never has time to talk to the patient to properly understand the problem. Instead the patient goes off to see experts to treat various symptoms. The system rarely deals with the cause of the problem. Once a symptom is dealt with the treatment is concluded till the next symptom appears.

One of the things I seriously dislike about our family court system is that life changing decisions have to be put in the hands of a legal representative who does not know the persons involved, and whom the persons concerned do not know. It is all in the lap of the Gods. If you happen to get a barrister or a judge on a bad day, your life can be ruined. Most legal representatives are not good across the whole range of topics in child matters. Your barrister may be good at negotiating with the other side or presenting the case to the judge, but he may be hopeless in asserting your position for reclaiming costs. The law is very complicated with lots of procedures and protocols. There are nasty legal traps for the uninitiated. If you are litigant in person you need to be good at talking in public, and to be assertive with a quick brain. An ability to read legal documents and case law at speed is also useful. For someone like me who hates to be reliant on other people the legal system is best avoided. Although I consider myself to be middle class, I acknowledge that my upbringing was in the advantaged spectrum of society. I noticed that the judges I went before were from similar or more advantaged backgrounds. In my childhood the Christian religion was an important element in private school education. We were brought up to view motherhood as portrayed by the Virgin Mary as sacrosanct. I postulate that amongst our judges, who are overwhelmingly male, there is a cultural bias born of their backgrounds to view motherhood as pure: certainly not possibly evil.

I also find the aura of secrecy that pervades the Family Court to be fundamentally misplaced. I have always believed that an adult should be responsible for his or her actions. If a man beats his wife then he should face the public's scorn. If that impacts on the childrens' attitude to him then so be it. Part of our society's problems lie in the refusal to blame or to hold people responsible for their actions. That element of reputation for most people acts as a curb on their behaviour. Most people do not want to be given a label of something scorned or shunned by society, so act to reduce that likelihood. If you are brought up to have a conscience, the sense of guilt can be very powerful. When things are proven in the Family court they should be available for common knowledge. In some circumstances, like mine, where the child is alienated, it should be possible to name and shame the adult responsible for that. The child would then at least have some idea of the truth from an official source. Public scorn is society's cheapest, swiftest, most profound deterrent for bad behaviour. My son is being brought up thinking his father is bad and his mother is wonderful. And the court is condoning that state of affairs. Charlie will hopefully learn the truth later in life. As a child he has the resilience to accept things and deal with them quickly. Knowing the truth now would be beneficial to Charlie. I would also prefer to name everyone in this book, but I am forbidden by the rules of secrecy till Charlie is 18 years old. I believe that public officials should be open to public criticism, and some named and shamed, just like rogue traders or miscreants from any other sector of society are. I do not have the money to continue legal proceedings or make complaints through the proper channels any more. My previous experience of complaining about a judge was a complete waste of time. I believe some people have been negligent, and others have failed Charlie. When Charlie is eighteen I shall consider publically criticising the officials that let Charlie down, and name and shame his mother for child abuse.

With the current levels of bias, incompetence and prohibitive costs I would advise any father in a similar situation to avoid using the courts. The best advice I was given was to keep a detailed diary. I wish on more occasions I had recorded how I actually felt too at the time. This is an area with no easy, useful advice but in my experience the court has made the situation much worse, put me through an emotional wringer and ruined me financially. What it has done to Charlie I can only guess, but I believe they are potentially devastating. But I remain confident that I did everything I could reasonably do for my son, short of getting into debt or going to prison. My conscience is clear and that is as important to me as my love for my son.

www.ingramcontent.com/pod-product-compliance
Ingram Content Group UK Ltd.
Pitfield, Milton Keynes, MK11 3LW, UK
UKHW040602210726
13854UKWH00008B/1839